MW00477756

Lose The Cape

*Cycle A Sermons Based on Second Lessons for Advent,
Christmas, and Epiphany*

Charley Reeb

CSS Publishing Company, Inc.

Lima, Ohio

LOSE THE CAPE

Cycle A Sermons Based on Second Lessons for Advent, Christmas, and Epiphany

FIRST EDITION
Copyright © 2019
by CSS Publishing Co., Inc.

Library of Congress Cataloging-in-Publication Data

Pending

For more information about CSS Publishing Company resources, visit our website at www.csspub.com, email us at csr@csspub.com, or call (800) 241-4056.

e-book:
ISBN-13: 978-0-7880-2992-9
ISBN-10: 0-7880-2992-4

ISBN-13: 978-0-7880-2991-2
ISBN-10: 0-7880-2991-6   PRINTED IN USA

In Memory of Art –
He was "all in."

Charly Reed

Contents

Preface

One of my mentors used to say, "Preachers would kill for a good story." He was prone to hyperbole, but he was right. After close to 25 years of pastoral ministry, I have learned there is often nothing more elusive than a good anecdote for a sermon and nothing more gratifying than finding one. This is why when I lead workshops and classes on preaching, I suggest to my students they keep a journal and write down any experience, conversation, or quote "that will preach." It takes some discipline but it more than pays off in the pulpit.

I have also learned after preparing countless sermons that you need some help from time to time finding good material. After all, what other profession requires you to prepare a keynote address every week? If you don't happen to have a staff of researchers and speech writers at your disposal, you must learn to be resourceful.

I hope this book in your hands will be a helpful resource for you as you prepare sermons. I have preached every message in this book and I am confident you will find some useful content. I was intentional about including stories, illustrations, quotes, and insights that would ease the burden of preparation and give you a little extra time to see a movie, hit golf balls or get lost in a novel. If anyone deserves some down time, it's a preacher!

Keep the faith and enjoy preaching it!

– Charley Reeb

Lose The Cape

When I was in college, I went to a friend's house for a pool party. I remember it being pretty tame by college standards. The parents were home! However, the dad of the house had a great personality. We told jokes, laughed and carried on.

Later in the evening, we were sitting by the pool and the father asked me what my major was. I told him it was religion. He laughed and said, "Yeah, right." I said, "No, I'm serious. It is religion." He asked, "Why religion?" I told him I planned on being a preacher. He said, "A what? You don't seem like any preacher I know (I took that as a compliment). You laugh and joke and have fun. You seem normal."

Before I left the party, he said something to me I will never forget: "I'm in my fifties and you are the first Christian I've ever met that I enjoy being around."

I don't tell you that story because I'm the hero — because, believe me, I've got a lot a work to do. I'm not always the hero in my stories! I tell you that story because the father at the party is not alone. There are people everywhere who have never had a positive experience of Christians.

Oliver Wendell Holmes once said, "I might have entered the ministry if certain clergymen I knew had not looked and acted so much like undertakers."

Robert Louis Stevenson once wrote in his diary, "I have been to church today, and am not depressed!"

Of course, Ghandi was famous for saying, "I like your Christ. It is Christians I have a problem with."

Shane Claiborne put it well: "Christianity has lost its fascination because it looks less and less like Jesus."

Sadly, when many of our friends, co-workers, and neighbors think of Christians, they don't think of Jesus, love or kindness. They think of people who are judgmental, opinionated, and hypocritical. Are we surprised there are so many empty pews?

As a Christian, have you ever thought about the kind of impression you make on others? What words would people use to describe you?

These are good questions to ask as we begin Advent. Many folks who don't go to church or claim a religion are yearning for the light and joy of the season. When they don't find it in the commercialization of Christmas, will they find it in those of us who claim to follow Christ and celebrate his birth?

The apostle Paul gave the following appeal:

It is now the moment for you to wake from sleep... Let us then lay aside the works of darkness and put on the armor of light (Romans 13:11-12 NRSV).

Jesus said something similar in Matthew:

"Let your light shine before others, that they may see your good deeds and glorify your Father in heaven" (Matthew 5:16 NIV).

Imagine if every Christians, in this world (that's 2.2 billion people, over 30% of the world's population) would get up every day, read these verses of scripture and say, "Today I am going to wear my armor of light. With every person I meet, in every circumstance I am in, I am going to let my light shine." Could you imagine what this world would be like? It would be a different world!

Unfortunately, for many Christians it is "lights out!" They have turned out their lights by favoring judgment over grace, hate over love, rules over relationships, dogma over forgiveness, and despair over hope.

I remember eating at an IHOP one morning. I was sitting in a booth facing a window that looked out at the parking lot. I watched as a car pulled in to a parking space. A woman and a man got out, and they were fighting with each other. I could not hear what they saying, but their body language said it all. I assumed they were married because they were fighting like a married couple. That is not a big deal. We all have our moments. But what was interesting about the lady is that she forgot what shirt she decided to put on that morning. Her T-shirt read, "Christ is Alive at … Community Church." Well, there was something alive in that woman that day, but I am not sure it was Jesus! Be careful of the T-shirts you wear and the bumper stickers you put on your car. Be sure you are living up to their messages!

Jesus didn't say, "Let your bad attitude show so that nobody in their right mind would want to be a Christian." Jesus said, "Let your light shine before others."

You know who understands this better than anyone? Children. They know how to let their light shine. That's why Jesus said that unless we can become like children we will never enter the kingdom of God.

My wife and I saw this message lived out when we were on a road trip a few years ago. We stopped at a pharmacy to grab some items for the road. We were in the checkout line when a grandmother and her four-year-old grandson walked into the store. Behind me was a big peanut "M&M" display. A yellow peanut "M&M" figure was holding up a big tray of candy. The four-year-old ran to the figure, which was about the same height as him, and smiled at it. He then threw his arms around it and said, "I love you!"

The whole place lit up! My wife and I laughed. The clerk laughed. All the people around us laughed. That child brightened the entire store! Walgreens never felt so happy. Kids know. "Put on the armor of light."

Unfortunately, Christians are known by a lot of things, but shining our light is way down on the list. Many Christians have forgotten to be the light! Have you? Now, I am not saying we have to be perfect, but we as Christians need to be doing a better job at shining our lights.

I remember when I was serving another church, a lady set an appointment with me. She was angry about something. Pastors love these appointments. She sat down in my office and said, "I have problems with some of your sermons." I replied, "Well, tell me. What's the problem?" She said, "You preach on love too much!" I said, "Well, before we go any further I want to suggest that you never say that to anyone else. You will not come across in a positive manner." She did not like that very well. She continued, "You preach on love too much. Where is the judgment? Where is the talk about sin?" I responded, "Well, I believe those subjects deserve study and attention, but last time I checked, Jesus said that the world will know we are his disciples if we have love for one another. And the Bible also says to let our let shine so we glorify our Father in heaven. He didn't tell us to let our judgment shine."

I would like to tell you that she had a change of heart, but she didn't. She stormed out of my office in anger. Sitting in judgment was more important to her than it was to Jesus.

When did Christians lose sight of the fact that we need to let our light shine? Tony Campolo tells the sad story from his high school days of how he failed to be a Christian. There was a boy in his class named Roger who was gay. He was tormented relentlessly by his classmates. They abused him emotionally and physically. One day, the abuse reached an unspeakable level. Five boys dragged Roger into the shower room, shoved him into the corner, and urinated all over him.

Around two o'clock the next morning, Roger went down into the basement of his house and hung himself.

When Campolo heard about it, he says he realized he wasn't a Christian. He knew all the right answers and could quote you chapter and verse of scripture, but he felt he hadn't live out his faith when it had come to Roger. If he had, he would have stood up for Roger and protected him. He would have been his friend. Perhaps that would have prevented him from taking his life (storiesforpreaching.com).

When did we as Christians lose our light? If you have lost your light, a great way to get it back is to reflect on these words of Jesus:

"You are the light of the world! A town built on a hill cannot be hidden. Neither do people light a lamp and put it under a bowl. Instead they put it on its stand, and it gives

light to everyone in the house. In the same way, let your light shine before others, that they may see your good deeds and glorify your Father in heaven." (Matthew 5:14-16 NIV)

I believe that in these verses Jesus is telling us that there is no such thing as a private Christian. We are called to stand out by letting our light shine. I also believe Jesus is reminding us that our light is attractive. The Christian faith is attractive. Our message is the most attractive message in the world! God created us, loves us, and wants a relationship with us. He wants us to share his love with the world! What is more attractive than that?

The late Aretha Franklin understood the attractiveness of God's light and love. She once said, "When God loves you, what can be better than that?" She was right. There is nothing better than that.

But there are a lot of people who don't know that love — who don't know they are loved. This is a cold, dark world and people are dying to see and feel our light. There are people who are wondering if the violence and evil around us is all there is. People desperately need love.

Growing up one of my favorite actors was Burt Reynolds. In the '70s and '80s, he owned Hollywood and had the world by the tail. He was in about half the movies that came out. Many people know, however, that Burt had his fair share of troubles in life. Drug abuse and relationship problems severely wounded him.

One night, I was staying in a hotel and couldn't sleep. I turned on the TV and there was Burt Reynolds being interviewed. He was being completely vulnerable about the source of pain in his life. His story is heart-wrenching. He said, "My dad never told me that he loved me. I would have given anything for him to tell me that he loved me, but he never did. At the end of his life, I thought he might say it -- but he never did." Can you imagine?

14

There are people you come across every day who are starving for love and light. They may look like they have it all together. They may be smiling, but inside they are desperate for compassion and love. What are we going to do about it?

Are you letting your light shine? Do you have on your "armor of light." If not, why not? Folks who are not Christians are watching us, wondering if our message has any credibility. If not, why should they bother with our faith? They don't expect us to be perfect, but they do expect to see some evidence that the light of Christ is real. How can they know unless we let it shine?

When Mister Rogers was a little boy and would see scary news on television, his mom would sit next to him, put her arms around him, and say, "Sweetheart, just look for the helpers. You will always find people who are helping. That will make you feel better."

In a world filled with hate, judgement, and violence, people are desperately looking for the helpers; the encouragers; the lovers — wondering if there is any hope.

Either we believe Jesus Christ is the help and hope of the world or we don't. Either we believe Jesus is the light of the world or we don't. Either we believe the light of Christ is within us or we don't.

The message of this sermon is simple: "Be the change you want to see in the world!" I don't know who said that, but they were right! As the old hymn says, "Let there be peace on earth, and let it begin with me!" Shine your light on someone. Encourage someone. Lift someone up. Write someone a kind note. Invite someone to church and take them to lunch. Call a loved one and tell them that you love them. Share your faith with a friend. Never underestimate the power of God's light within you. Booker T. Washington said, "If you want to lift yourself up, lift up someone else."

Have you ever seen the movie *The Incredibles*? It's about a family of superheroes who tries to save the world from total destruction. In Bob Goff's book *Love Does*, he writes about the superhero dad in the movie. The dad is an insurance claims adjustor, but he really wants to use his superhero powers, so he begins drawing pictures of the superhero suits he wants to wear. Of course, all the suits include capes.

The dad has a friend named Edna who makes superhero suits, and she keeps telling him that he needs to lose the cape. She tells him how in the end, capes cause big problems for superheroes. They get caught on things like gates or jet engines. Edna says in the movie, "No capes!" You get a lot more stuff done if you lose the cape.

Bob Goff thinks Jesus agrees with Edna, and so do I! You know what I think will draw the world to Christ and leave a good taste in people's mouths about religion? It will be when Christians lose the cape. So many of us who follow Christ do it with a cape representing something — a cape to be noticed by others so they will think we are so good; a cape representing something we are against or some judgment we hold for certain people; a cape symbolizing our denomination, political views, or our interpretation of scripture. Soon we become known by our capes and not by Jesus. Our capes hide our light (Bob Goff, *Love Does*, Nashville, Thomas Nelson Publishers, 2012, page 159).

Another problem is that if we go around serving Jesus with capes, they eventually get snagged on something — our pride; other people's feelings; people's perceptions of those who follow God. Our capes get in the way.

Goff reminds us that Jesus never wore a cape. Jesus hardly ever talked about the way he loved people. He just did it. All that mattered to him was that God knew it. When we lose the cape, we don't get confused about what our purpose is, which is to love. All our energy is channeled into doing great things for God and loving the world like crazy (Goff).

Let's lose the cape as Christians and just go out and share the light and love of Jesus. When we serve Jesus without a cape people will want to know more about Jesus. This Advent season let us put on the armor of light and draw people to the light of the world.

Amen.

*(Portions of this sermon were preached on Day1: http://day1.org/8293-charley_reeb_lose_the_cape)

Find Joy Again!

There are many hysterical stories associated with my parents and family. There is one that has been the source of great laughter over the years. The event occurred one weekend when my parents drove me to a tennis tournament in another city. After my match, I was hungry, so my dad drove us to Shoney's. I don't know if they are still around, but they used to have a big breakfast buffet.

My dad loved to eat. It was a real hobby for him. As a result, he had the "Dunlop" disease. His belly "dunlopped" over his belt. Whenever he sat down to eat, he would often unbutton his pants so his belly could breathe. This day at Shoney's was no different. He happily brought back two plates of food to the table, unbuttoned his pants, and commenced eating. When he finished, he picked up the two plates and went back to the buffet for seconds. However, he had forgotten to do one very important thing -- button up his pants. So, halfway to the buffet -- in front of God and everybody -- my dad's pants fell down to his ankles! There he was in the middle of Shoney's, sporting his tighty whities. My mom turned purple with laughter. I also noticed a lady near my dad spit out her pancakes in horror. I am just glad he was wearing underwear that day! I was a teenage kid at the time, and I am still scarred by it.

My dad could not use his hands because he was holding two plates, so the only thing he could do was shuffle his way back to the table. When he got to the table, he threw down the plates and said to us, "I'll be in the car!"

I don't know if that Shoney's still exists. They may have gone out of business the next day. If they are still around, I am sure they are still talking about the man who dropped his pants in the middle of the restaurant.

Such laughter and fun has always been a part of my family history. I love to laugh, and you need to know that I have a very loud laugh. I do a lot of things loud. If I think something is funny, I really think it is funny! And that is a good thing, I guess, because someone once said that the sound of heaven is not singing but laughter.

The holiness of laughter reminds me of a story about C.S. Lewis. A group of theologians and scholars approached the great Christian thinker and asked him, "What is the most important theological discovery you have ever made?" Lewis smiled and responded, "I exist to enjoy God's enjoyment of me."

Did you hear that? God enjoys you! God wants you to enjoy him, to enjoy life, and to enjoy the world he has created.

Scripture backs up God's call to enjoy life. Paul gives us this blessing:

> May the God of hope fill you with all joy and peace in believing, so that you may abound in hope by the power of the Holy Spirit (Romans 15:13 NRSV).

Also consider these words from Paul:

Command those who are rich in this present world not to be arrogant nor to put their hope in wealth, which is so uncertain, but to put their hope in God, who richly provides us with everything for our enjoyment(1 Timothy 6:17 NIV).

A long, long time ago, a group of people in the church got together and thought it was important to list the most important beliefs of Christianity. They called it a "catechism." But they soon discovered that the list was too long and difficult to memorize, so they came up with a "short catechism." This was to be a summary of the key beliefs of our faith. Do you know how this shorter catechism begins? "What is the chief end of humankind? To glorify God and enjoy him forever!"

Ironically, I come across many people who won't allow God into their lives because they think God is going to make them give up fun. Many misguided Christians have perpetuated this nonsense. They give off the impression that to become a Christian means the party is over -- that being spiritual means being miserable.

Nothing could be further from the truth. In fact, to become a Christian means the party is just beginning. When you have the joy of Christ in your heart you can't help but smile and have a good time. After all, God created joy and fun. It was his idea! The closer we get to God, the more joy we have.

God created us to play and to enjoy the life he created. I believe one of the reasons Christians and churches burn out is they lose their sense of play. They lose their joy. Jesus tells us so. Remember that scene in the gospels when Jesus was teaching while a bunch of playful kids ran toward him? The sour disciples were appalled. You can imagine their reaction. "Children ought to be seen and not heard. Where are their parents? Can't they see these kids are interrupting Jesus? Get these kids out of here!"

The Bible says that Jesus became very angry at the disciples. He was appalled at the way the disciples were treating the kids. He said, "What are you doing? Let the children come to me. Don't get in their way. In fact, unless you can receive the kingdom like these kids, you will never be able to enter it."

I have always thought that was an amazing statement from Christ. But having a child of my own has helped me to truly understand and experience its meaning. Children are receptive, dependent, and trusting. They bring nothing but themselves and their joy. Jesus says that unless we are able to receive God and his kingdom like that, we will never understand what it means to live for God.

It has been said that "God is happiest when his children are at play." I believe that. The most beautiful sound in the world to me is the sound of my son Paul's laughter. It goes straight to my soul and often brings me to tears. Now, if I receive that much joy from my son's laughter and joy, imagine how much joy God receives from the laughter and joy of all his children.

I was reminded of this one day when I was playing with my son at the pool. We were bouncing him up and down in the water. I closed my eyes and listened to the children laughing, splashing, and playing. I thought, "This is the sound of the kingdom."

G.K. Chesterton wrote, "God is the last child left in the universe." He said the rest of us have just lost our joy. I have thought a lot about those words, and I believe Chesterton was on to something. When we read Genesis, we see that joy radiated through God as he created the universe. When God created you and me, there was great joy in his heart.

Tony Campolo talks about the time when his grandson was just a little boy and he would play with him on his knee. He would bounce him up and down, lift him up into the air, and bring him down to the floor. Campolo said that every time he would do this his grandson would say, "Do it again, Pop! Do it again!" And Campolo would do it again. Of course, his grandson would say to him once more, "Do it again, Pop! Do it again!"

Campolo says that when God created that first daisy, something childlike inside the heart of God said, "Do it again! Do it again!" And after the fourth and fifth daisy, God said to himself, "Do it again! Do it again!" And after the 50 billionth, trillionth daisy, God was jumping up and down, clapping his hands saying, "Do it again! Do it again!" We have a God of joy, fun, and play. (Campolo, *Let Me Tell You a Story*, pages 12 and 13, Nashville, Word Publishing, 2000.)

But something happened to our world. We lost our joy. We lost our sense of fun and laughter. Sin and cynicism crept in and caused us to lose our ability to play. God wanted us to get our joy back, so he decided to come to us in Jesus Christ. One of the things God said to us in Jesus was;

> *"I have come that they might have life and have it in all of it abundantly!"* (John 10:10 TLV)

In Jesus, God was showing us his joyful personality so that we would get our joy back. At first, the world really did not know how to respond to this. We see an example of it in Luke 7 when Jesus spoke to the Pharisees, the supposed experts of the Jewish Law. They thought they knew everything there was to know about God. Jesus comes along and says, "You just don't get it. I come eating, drinking, and having a good time -- and you accuse me of being a glutton, drunkard, and a friend to sinners and tax collectors." They accused Jesus of being a party animal. They thought he was playing too hard. They thought they had God all figured out, but they hadn't. They could not see that Jesus was trying to get us to enjoy life again.

Do you know what Jesus' first miracle was in John? It occurred in a small town called Cana at a wedding party. Now, a wedding party back then could go on for an entire week! Imagine getting that bill! Jesus was invited to this party. So, I want you to appreciate this. One of the first scenes of Jesus in John is not him teaching in the plains or holding a sick person's hand; it is Jesus at a party!

Well, after a few days, they ran out of wine. What do you think Jesus did? Help clean up and say goodnight? No! He told some folks to fill several large jars with water and he performed his first miracle by turning all that water into wine. Jesus' first miracle in John was not healing the sick, feeding the hungry, walking on water, or raising the dead. His first miracle was creating about 180 gallons of wine on the spot so a party could continue!

The meaning of the miracle is not that Jesus is thrilled when we get intoxicated. It is about the extravagant joy and love Jesus came to bring us. You can read the story of Jesus turning the water into wine over and over again. You can send it to scholars and theologians trying to find some profound meaning, but you will never find it. The great truth of that story is this: Sometimes, Jesus did things for fun! Jesus was showing us how to get our joy back and for our joy to be full.

I think of it this way: When I was a little boy and would get grumpy and grouchy, my dad had a clever way of changing my mood. He would not lecture me. He wouldn't tell me that I should be grateful for what I had and not complain. He would get on the floor with me and find a place just above my belly button and blow air bubbles on my tummy. He would do it until I smiled and gave in to laughter. Quite simply, this is what God did for us in Jesus. God got down on our level and embraced us so that we would find joy again.

So, you have homework to do. Go out and let yourself be loved. Go hack at a golf ball. Take dance lessons and learn how to dance. Turn on your favorite song and sing like no one is watching or listening. Watch your favorite comedy again for the twentieth time and laugh your way to joy!

I came across a wonderful quote from Nadine Stair, an 85-year-old woman from the hill country of Kentucky:

"If I had to live my life over again, I would dare to make more mistakes next time. I would relax. I would be sillier... I've been one of those persons who never went anyplace without a thermometer, a hot water bottle, a raincoat, and a parachute. If I had to do it over again, I'd travel lighter."

What would you say if you had to finish this sentence: "If I had to live my life over, I would ..."? Don't wait to experience God's joy in your life. Do it now! Learn to play again. Enjoy God's enjoyment of you. Remember Paul's words:

May the God of hope fill you with all joy and peace in believing, so that you may abound in hope by the power of the Holy Spirit (Romans 15:13 NRSV).

Amen!

Inside Out

Harvard University once revoked their acceptance of ten incoming students because of inappropriate content they had posted on Facebook. A description of the Harvard College Class official Facebook group states, "Harvard College reserves the right to withdraw an offer of admission ... if an admitted student engages in behavior that brings into question his or her honesty, maturity, or moral character."

A recent study showed that over 40% of colleges and universities look at the Facebook pages and other social media accounts of prospective students.

The lesson: You really can't hide who you are. Eventually, who you are will be revealed, so be vigilant about protecting your character. I believe this is what the writer of James had in mind when he wrote:

> *Be patient and stand firm, because the Lord's coming is near. Don't grumble against one another, brothers and sisters, or you will be Judged. The judge is standing at the door!* (James 5:8-9 NIV).

A pastor once invited a man in the congregation to join him up on the platform during his sermon. He handed the man a glass of water filled to the top. As the pastor continued to preach, he bumped the man's arm and water spilled onto the pastor. The pastor turned to the man and asked, "Why did you spill water on me?" The man replied, "Because you bumped into me." The pastor said, "I know I bumped you, but why did you spill water on me?" The man replied, "Uh, I spilled water on you because you bumped my arm." "Let me put it this way: Why did you spill water on me? Why didn't you spill coffee, lemonade or tomato juice?" The man concluded, "Because that's what was in the glass — just water."

The pastor then turned to his congregation and said that every day we fill ourselves with good character choices and bad character choices. Inevitably, life is going to bump us around and provoke what's inside of us to spill out. What will spill out of you? Will it be fear or confidence; generosity or greed? Will it be humility or pride? What do you want to reveal to others (Ben Decker and Kelly Decker, *Communicate to Influence: How to Inspire Your Audience to Action* (New York: McGraw Hill, 2015), ch. 5, Kindle)?

That pastor was right. Life has a way of revealing what's on the inside of us. Sooner or later in life, something will bump you around and reveal what you are made of. So, the next time you hit a bump in the road, what will spill out of you?

The Bible is clear about what should spill out of us. It is called the fruit of the Spirit:

> *But the fruit of the Spirit is love, joy, peace, forbearance, kindness, goodness, faithfulness, gentleness and self-control* (Galatians 5:22-23 NIV).

As followers of Christ, these are the qualities or virtues that should spill out of us. Of course, if we make bad choices or dwell on bad thoughts, something else might spill out.

Did you watch Sesame Street growing up? If so, you know about Oscar the Grouch. He has a terrible attitude and insults everyone. As they say, "Garbage in, garbage out."

It's interesting how Oscar the Grouch got his name. King Duncan writes, "In the early days of Sesame Street, Jim Henson and Jon Stone, Sesame Street's directors, would meet to work on the upcoming show at a Manhattan restaurant. The name of the restaurant was Oscar's Cavern. Each time they ate there, they were waited on by a man who was consistently rude and grouchy. The result was that the waiter's attitude was forever immortalized on Sesame Street in the character of Oscar the Grouch" (from Duncan's sermon "Positive Living" — https://sermons. com/sermon/positive-living/1442666).

Do any of you know a grouch? They are not fun to be around, are they? They can suck the life and joy right out of you.

Fortune magazine published an article with a list of some actual lines that people had written in resumes and cover letters:

"It's best for employers that I not work with people." Would you want to hire that applicant?

"I have become completely paranoid, trusting completely no one and absolutely nothing."

"Note: Please don't misconstrue my [previous] 14 jobs as 'job-hopping.' I have never quit a job." Does this mean he was fired from 14 jobs?

"The company made me a scapegoat, just like my three previous employers [did]" (quotes from Duncan's sermon, "Positive Living").

I don't know about you, but I would put those letters and resumes in the trash and start looking for people to hire who have these qualities: "love, joy, peace, patience, kindness, goodness, faithfulness, gentleness, and self-control."

Ever been around someone who exudes the fruits of the spirit? They make your day, don't they?

Duncan observes that "none of these characteristics that Paul lists as fruit of the Spirit depends on external circumstance. No matter what happens to you from the outside, you can still possess love, joy, peace, patience, kindness, goodness, faithfulness, gentleness, and self-control" on the inside (Duncan).

"The Irish tenor Ronan Tynan had both legs amputated below the knee after a motorbike accident many years ago. How would you react to such misfortune? I'll tell you how Tynan responded. He went on to become a medical doctor, a well-known Irish tenor, and an excellent athlete. In the 1984 and 1988 paralympics, he won four gold medals in the discus, the shot put, and the long jump. He even rode show horses. A tall man, he had a special set of artificial legs made for riding. He became an equestrian master. A reporter once asked Tynan, 'How tall are you, really?' Tynan replied, 'I'm adjustable'" (Duncan, "Positive Living").

I love it! What a great attitude! Most of us would become grouches if we lost our legs. Tynan certainly had every excuse to become one. Instead, he chose to be adjustable. He knew he had a choice about the kind of person he became and the attitude he embraces.

Are you adjustable to life? When something bad happens, do you play the victim or do you stay faithful, knowing God will redeem your suffering? When someone is mean to you, do you get even, or do you choose to be kind instead? When the world is full of hate, do you show the world a better way and love instead?

There is a reason why Paul puts love at the top of the list. Love is what opens up the rest of the fruit. But it is not just any kind of love. The word love Paul uses here is seen about 540 times in the Bible. In the Old Testament, it is the word, "hesed." In the New Testament it is "agape." Agape is self-giving love; a sacrificial love; an unconditional love — a love that works in the best interest of others regardless of how we may feel about them — a love that sacrifices for others regardless of what they have done to us. It is the word used to describe the unconditional love of God.

Agape is love in action. It is an action word. That's why Paul chooses to define this love through action words. What does this love look like? It is patient. It is kind. It is selfless. It is faithful, gentle, and kind. It is humble. It is forgiving. It rejoices in the truth. It always protects, trusts, hopes, and perseveres. In other words, true Christian love is not something you talk about or think about; it is something you do!

Agape love is also a decision. It is not based on feelings. Although right feelings often come after we express this love, agape love is choosing to love regardless of how you may feel. When that guy cuts you off, you choose to be patient and not give him a particular kind of wave. When the waitress gets your order wrong, you choose to be kind, loving, and tip her well, regardless. When you see the homeless man, you choose to not to be judgmental or critical but to see him with the eyes of Christ and recognize his worth. When you see the old couple walking slowly down the cereal aisle, you choose to be patient and kind. Perhaps they just came from the doctor and received a bad pathology report. These are the few precious moments they have together. When five o'clock rolls around and you are tired and ready to go home, you stay a little longer to listen to a co-worker who is upset. When people betray you, you choose not to retaliate but forgive because you know that is what Christ did for you.

Agape love -- Christian love; the love of God revealed in Jesus Christ -- is what will heal this word. This love is the acid test of being a follower of Jesus. The central thrust of Jesus' teaching and ministry was that sacrificial love wins, and forgiving enemies overthrows evil. This is the power of the cross. If we don't believe this, we are just another charity organization.

Let's face it: Every other group in society can do everything else Christians do. Christians have programs. So does every other group. We recite creeds. So, do many other groups like the Rotary and Kiwanis clubs. Christians sing songs. So does every other group. Christians raise money. So does every other group.

So what makes us different? What makes us unique? What do we as Christ followers do that is different from any other non-profit organization? We love unconditionally! We forgive our enemies! We love sacrificially! We do not return evil for evil but choose to do good when evil is done to us. We do what is best for another, regardless of who they are or what they have done. We see others not as the world sees them but as children of God who have sacred worth.

Harold Warlick said, "The greatness of our faith is our expansive loving spirit that overthrows resentments, takes in enemies, embraces rivals, and seeks the best for everyone."

Let's bring this down to a personal level. On a general level, agape love is fairly easy to take -- but what about our personal relationships?

Reverend James Moore recalls visiting a woman who was dying in a local hospital. She was in her mid-sixties. Her son flew in to be with her. Moore was there when he arrived and entered the room. He walked over to the bedside of his dying mother, leaned over, and kissed her on the cheek. He was so moved by how weak she was that he said, "Mom, you have been such a good mother to me. And, I want you to know I love you."

The mother started to cry; and through her tears, she said: "Son, that's the first time you've ever told me. Last Friday was your sixty-third birthday and that's the first time you ever told me." Moore comments by saying, "Isn't that something? It took him 63 years to say, 'I love you' to his mother" (James Moore, "A Mother's Love" — https://sermons.com/sermon/a-mother-s-love/1357866).

Is there someone you need to express your love to today? Don't wait! Do it now! If your parents are still living, when was the last time you told them you love and appreciate them? When was the last time you told your spouse, family, and friends that you love them? When was the last time you told your children how proud you are of them? When was the last time you loved someone by spending time with them?

Are you estranged from a loved one? Forgive them as Christ has forgiven you. Life is too short -- and Christ calls us to take the first step because that is what he did for all of us. Your forgiving love will bring healing to you and perhaps healing to the one you are forgiving. Agape love is powerful and transforming.

Leo Buscalgia was a famous writer and speaker who traveled around the world and talked about one important subject: love. When he finished speaking, there was usually a long line of people waiting to hug him. Buscalgia says that most of them were not waiting in line to talk to him, but to simply receive a hug. He said he would come across so many people who told him that they have not been hugged or touched in years. They walked away from the encounter new people (http://www.buscaglia.com/biography).

When we know we are loved, we can do anything; conquer anything; overcome anything! The Apostle Paul said it best in Romans 8:37: "We are more than conquerors through Christ who loves us."

The love of God always wins. This is the essence of our faith and what the gospels teach us over and over again. Jesus sums it up by telling us that the world will know we are Christians by our love — not by the way we worship; not by our knowledge of the Bible; not by our sophisticated theology; not by our judgments; not by our denomination; but by our love for each other!

In John 15, Jesus underscores the fruit of the Spirit by telling us that his purpose for us is that we bear much fruit. And what is that fruit supposed to be? It's the one that's listed first in Galatians:

"My command is this: Love each other as I have loved you. Greater love has no one than this: to lay down one's life for one's friends" (John 15:12-13 NIV).

Now, most of us are not going to be called to die for another, but all of us are called to love in some way. For most us, this means sacrificing time — helping someone with a flat tire, baking cookies for a new neighbor, listening to someone when you would be rather be home watching television, or throwing the ball with your child when you would rather take a nap. In the end, those are the moments that count.

Oh how we need to learn this lesson! I can't tell you how many people I have visited and how many people who have crossed the threshold of my office door who wished they had lived lives motivated by love. They talk about the times spent arguing about trivial matters. They talk of the energy spent resenting. They talk about the money wasted on needless things and the time wasted on a ridiculous pursuit. They wish they had learned the importance of love earlier.

I have done many funerals in my ministry. You know what I have never heard at a funeral? I have never heard anyone mention how much money the deceased person had in their bank account when they died. No one has ever mentioned how many houses or boats they owned; or their golf handicap. You know what has been mentioned? The love they shared with others — the laughter and joy they shared with family and friends — the transforming moments.

When a pastor discusses your funeral with your family, what will they say about you? What will really matter to them? Have you ever thought about that? What will matter to them will be how well you loved. Our lives will be measured by how well we loved. Love never fails! Everything else will cease. Everything else will pass away. These three remain: faith, hope, and love -- and the greatest of these is love.

What is on the inside of you can be seen on the outside. Is your life revealing the fruit of the Spirit?

Some of you may feel discouraged when you review the fruit of the Spirit because you feel like it is impossible to reflect all of these qualities. You are right! It is impossible without God's help. That's why they are called the fruit of the Spirit. If we want to bear fruit, we must first have the Spirit of God living within us. Jesus said, "Apart from me, you can do nothing."

King Duncan writes about a girl who sang in the choir of a church in East London:

"She had this wonderful voice, but she had also been well-trained in vocal technique. Her fame as a soloist spread until one Christmas, she was invited to sing one of the lead parts in "Messiah" at the Queen's Hall.

"One of her closest friends went to her teacher, asking whether he thought she was equal to the task. His response was this: 'If she focuses on what I have tried to teach her and merely follows the rules of correct breathing and voice production, she will break down. But if she can forget everything and think only of the wonder of the message she is singing, she will be all right.'

"The night came. This lovely young woman stepped forward and began singing, 'I know that my Redeemer liveth.' The music flowed in great beauty from her lips. And the best hopes of her teacher were fulfilled. She forgot the audience and the occasion, and sang as one who knew the meaning of it all. She sang in the strength of the living Christ whom she knew intimately and who was in power within her own life. As she sang, the audience was strangely moved. That night was one to be remembered. Why? Because she was not trying merely to follow directions or obey a set of external rules; she had found a Spirit of power, within." She sang the message, not just the notes (Duncan, "Positive Living").

I teach the same principle to my preaching students. Many of them will get very concerned about proper delivery or memorizing material. I tell them that the key to great preaching is conviction. If your message is coming from the bottom of your heart, your delivery will take care of itself. You will also not have to worry about remembering anything because you will be preaching "by heart."

The same principle applies to our faith. Is the Spirit inside of you? When it is, you will not be concerned about doing everything right but rather doing everything by heart. You will not be following rules but following the guidance of the Holy Spirit. This is when you reflect the fruit of the Spirit and make a difference in this world for Christ.

Amen.

Why Christianity?

I went to Florida Southern College in Lakeland, Florida. It was a wonderful experience. After seminary, I was appointed as an associate pastor at First UMC of Lakeland and had a good relationship with the college. In fact, one of my favorite professors once invited me to be a guest speaker in his class. It was a sociology class, and they were studying religion and society. He wanted a local pastor to come and speak about the church and community. I was still a little wet behind the ears, but I thought I did a pretty good job explaining my role and answering questions.

As the class was wrapping up, there was a student in the back of the class who raised her hand high. I called on her and she asked, "Why are you a Christian?" I replied, "Excuse me?" She repeated, "Why are you a Christian? I am taking a class in world religions and there are so many beautiful religions in the world. Why did you choose to be a Christian minister?"

Do you know why you are a Christian? If someone were to ask you why you follow Jesus rather than a zillion other religions and philosophies out there, what would you say? Would you be able to give a solid answer? Would your answer be convincing?

The apostle Paul was absolutely convinced of the truth of Christ. He wrote:

Paul, a servant of Christ Jesus, called to be an apostle and set apart for the gospel of God — the gospel he promised beforehand through his prophets in the Holy Scriptures regarding his Son, who as to his earthly life was a descendant of David, and who through the Spirit of holiness was appointed the Son of God in power by his resurrection from the dead: Jesus Christ our Lord (Romans 1:1-4 NIV).

Paul was extremely confident in his faith. There was a time when I envied having that kind of faith. Oh, I grew up in the church. I sang "Jesus loves me." I accepted Jesus Christ as my Lord and Savior at a young age, and was baptized. But when I entered my teenage years and began thinking critically, I wondered: If I had been born into a different religion would I have still chosen to follow Jesus?

What makes Christianity so special? Why should people follow Jesus instead of the thousands of religions out in the world? There are roughly 4,200 religions in the world. Really! No joke. Why should Christianity be any different than the rest of them? Are we the only ones who are right?

Maybe some of you have asked the same question. In the back of your mind you have often wondered why you follow Jesus instead of another religion. Is it because you were born into a Christian home? Maybe a professor challenged you, or skeptical friends said something, or you watched a documentary on world religions and have often wondered about the validity of your faith ever since.

Perhaps you are someone who has always been on the edge of becoming a Christian. You want to follow Jesus, but the one obstacle for you has been the question, "Why

Jesus instead of another religion?"

This message is going to tell you why. At the end of this sermon, you will be able to tell your skeptical friends a compelling reason why you are a Christian. If you are someone still searching for faith, this message just may be the tipping point for you.

When I began to ask these questions as a teenager, it sent me on an obsessive quest to find an answer. Through much prayer, study, and research, I made a discovery that not only moved me to recommit myself to Christ but was also instrumental to my call to ministry.

What is so unique and compelling about the Christian faith? And why should it make any difference to your life? I am going to let the gospel of John tell you. We usually turn to Matthew and Luke for the Christmas story — the shepherds, the angels, Mary and Joseph, and the birth of Jesus. John doesn't include any of that. Instead, John gets right to the point and explains *why* Jesus is compelling and life changing:

> *In the beginning was the Word, and the Word was with God, and the Word was God. He was with God in the beginning. Through him all things were made; without him nothing was made that has been made* (John 1:1-3 NIV).

What is John talking about? He is talking about Jesus. Substitute *Word* with *Jesus*. Why wouldn't John just write Jesus? Because John is trying to tell us something unique about Jesus. *Word* means the essence of God or God's personality. Jesus is God's personality. In the beginning was God's personality, and it was God's personality that made the world. Take a look at what it says next:

In him was life, and that life was the light of all mankind. The light shines in the darkness, and the darkness has not overcome it. The true light that gives light to everyone was coming into the world (John 1:4-5, 9 NIV).

God's Word, God's personality, is filled with light and life. You've heard of people who light up a room. God's personality lights up the world! And that light is so strong that nothing, not even darkness, can kill it. But notice what happens:

He was in the world, and though the world was made through him, the world did not recognize him. He came to that which was his own, but his own did not receive him (John 1:10, 11 NIV).

Here's the sad thing. John was telling us that even though God's personality is filled with light and love, some people are not going to recognize it, understand it, or receive it.

But here is what happens to us if we are open to experiencing God's personality:

Yet to all who did receive him, to those who believed in his name, he gave the right to become children of God (John 1:12 NIV).

Those who were open to understanding and experiencing God's personality and light will be transformed by it. How is that possible? Take a look:

The Word became flesh and made his dwelling among us. We have seen his glory, the glory of the one and only Son, who came from the Father, full of grace and truth (John 1:14 NIV).

And there it is! God's personality took human form 2,000 years ago in the person of Jesus of Nazareth. God's personality has always existed, but that personality intersected human history when Jesus was born!

So why does John say some people will not recognize it or receive it? Because God showed up in a way no one expected. He wasn't born in a palace. His parents were not royalty. There was no earthquake that announced his coming. He was born in a dirty feeding trough inside a cold cave to poor peasant parents. Other than a few shepherds and some astrologists, no one had a clue God had shown up.

Why did God choose to display his personality this way? He made that choice because if he had been royalty, he would have been untouchable. If he had come with great fanfare, we would have been intimidated. If he came swooping in on a high horse, he would have been unrelatable. But being a little baby born in a humble manner — now that warms our heart. There is nothing more disarming than a precious baby.

I think of when my son Paul was born. I just fell to pieces. I felt such love; my heart was so open. I had so much love to give. If you had asked me that day to give you all the money in my bank account, I would have done it! Of course, all first-time parents feel that way, but it was extra special for us because we were told for eighteen years we could never have children. God had different plans. He is our miracle baby. Our little baby has changed our lives. A baby has a way of doing that.

One night, we were at a restaurant with Paul and he was getting restless. Brandy and I were taking turns holding him so we could eat. Near our table, there was a bar filled with people. They were loud and cynical. Not a lot of smiles. But when Brandy walked Paul near the bar so he could see the boats outside, the people around the bar lit up! Their frowns turned into smiles and they reached out to play with Paul's rock star hair! They were transformed. There was life in their eyes. A baby does that to people.

You know what? Baby Jesus did that for the whole world! He gave life and love to the world. It was the best way God could convey how much he loves us and wants a relationship with us. Nobody in the history of humankind changed things the way that baby did. Jesus had the most humble beginning, the most humiliating ending, and yet the biggest impact the earth has ever seen. You see, it had to start like this — we had to see that God gets us — that he is with us.

So why is Jesus so compelling? Why does Jesus and the Christian faith stand out for me? Why do I love being a follower of Jesus? Because *religion is reaching for God; Christianity (Jesus) is God reaching for us.* This is exactly what I told the student that day in class (Charley Reeb, *Say Something: Simple Ways to Make Your Sermons Matter*, Nashville: Abingdon Press, 2019, forthcoming).

Christianity means we don't have to search for God. Instead God searches for us and finds us. No other religion in the world makes this claim. In every other religion, people are desperately seeking to find God or the divine. There is beauty and truth in many of them. But in the Christian faith, a faith unlike any other, God finds us in the person of Jesus Christ. God seeks us out. And, to be honest, there's really no other way we could find our way.

Author Max Lucado told about a trip his family took to the United Kingdom. They visited a castle. In the center of the castle garden was a large maze of shoulder-high hedges. It was a labyrinth of dead ends. If you are able to find your way out of the labyrinth, there is a door to a tall tower in the center of the garden.

Lucado said that if you were to look at their family pictures of the trip, you'd see four of their five family members standing on the top of the tower. Guess who was missing? That's right. Lucado was stuck in that maze. He couldn't figure out which way to go. But then he heard a voice from above. "Hey, Dad." He looked up and saw his daughter Sara looking down on him. "You're going the wrong way," she explained. "Back up and turn right."

Do you think he trusted her? He didn't have to. He could have trusted his own instincts, asked other lost travelers, or sat and complained about why he couldn't find his way. But do you know what he did? He listened. Her perspective was better than his. She was above the maze. She could see what he couldn't (https://maxlucado. com/listen/out-of-the-maze/).

It's the same way with us. We don't know where we are going. Trying to find or figure out God is like getting lost in that maze. There are so many options, so many opinions. Which way do we go? Who do we listen to? We could never figure it out. It's beyond us. That's why we need someone from above who can show us the way. And that is exactly why God came to us in Jesus. He came down to find us and point us the way home.

If that doesn't hit home, let me ask you this question: What would the world be like if Jesus had never been born? Ever thought of it that way? Imagine this world if Jesus had never been born.

Many atheists claim that faith and religion are bad for the world. Well, they just haven't thought through it. Do you know what would be missing in this world if Jesus had never been born? No Christmas cards, caroling or concerts. No Christmas gift giving, candlelights, or twinkling trees. But also no Valentine's Day, St. Patrick's Day, Easter, Halloween, or Thanksgiving. Each one of those holidays is based on or tied to Christianity. But that is just on the surface. Reflecting on this question, Greg Asimakoupoulos writes:

If Jesus had never been born, we would not have the sermon on the mount... Can you imagine a world without Handel's Messiah?... Can you imagine a world without the Hallelujah Chorus?... Can you imagine a world without Bonhoeffer and those who stood against Hitler?... Can you imagine a world without Billy Graham's Crusades, Martin Luther King's Christian movement against racism, or Mother Theresa's Christlike compassion to the poor and dying?... Most of all, can you imagine living in a world without knowing God is love, approachable, and compassionate, or living in a world without the assurance that we have been forgiven and redeemed? (Finding God in *"It's a Wonderful Life,"* eChristian Books: https://www.amazon.com/Finding-God-Its-Wonderful-Life/dp/1618433059, 2012, Kindle Version).

If Jesus did that for the world, imagine what he can do for your life! Jesus is not a gift we find, but a gift that finds us! Imagine what your life would be missing without him. Or maybe I should say: Imagine what your life *is* missing without him.

You see, although Jesus searches and finds us, we still have to invite him in. That's another reason why God was born a baby. A baby is not forceful. A baby does not insist on being held. You must invite him into your life. Embrace God's embrace of you in Christ.

I recall being in seminary serving as a hospital chaplain at Emory hospital. This was a great way to train ministers. "You want to go into the ordained ministry? Serve the sick and the dying and you will find out what real ministry is."

I was doing my rounds one day. It was my first year of seminary. I was naïve and nervous. I had a badge on my coat that said "clergy," but most of the time I forgot I was wearing it. A nurse called out, "Chaplain?" I turned around to look for the chaplain and then realized she was talking to me! She said, "You see that man in that room over there? His name is Walter. He is not doing well at all, and no one has come by to see him. Would you mind visiting with him?" I said, "Sure." As I walked toward the room, the nurse said, "Oh, and one more thing — Walter is a very angry man."

I walked into the room and said, "Hello, Walter. My name is Charley Reeb, and I am one of the chaplains here. He replied, "You are, are you? Well, I do not need a chaplain, and I don't need God. Just get out of here!" I said, "Well, do you need a friend?" He said, "I don't need anybody. Just leave me alone." I proceeded to walk out of the door and before I put my hand on the door he cried out, "I haven't always been this way, you know! I had life by the tail. Then this cancer got ahold of me and tore me apart..." He went on and on, and I just listened.

When Walter finished talking I asked, "Do you mind if I say a prayer for you?" He replied, "I don't think it will do any good, but you go right ahead." In the middle of my prayer, I asked God to cover Walter in his loving arms like a warm blanket. When I finished my prayer, I could not believe what I saw. There were tears coming down Walter's cheeks, and his arms were up in the air, ready for a hug. I reached down and put my arms around his fragile body, and he began to rock me back and forth, repeating the words, "Cover me like a blanket. Cover me like a blanket."

I had no control over what occurred that day, but God's power and love made my prayer become flesh for Walter. Christ worked through me to reach out to Walter. Religion is reaching for God; Christianity is God reaching for us (Charles Reeb, *One Heaven of a Party*, Lima, Ohio: CSS Publishing Company, 2003, pages 107-109).

Amen.

*(Part of this sermon was preached on Day1 — http:// day1.org/8295-charley_reeb_why_christianity. This is my work.)

Get The Grinch

I have wonderful news for you! Because of a brave little boy from Mississippi, the Grinch will not steal your Christmas. 5-year-old TyLon Pittman called 911 and said to the dispatcher, "I just want to tell you something. Watch for that little Grinch because the Grinch is gonna steal Christmas, okay?"

When police officer Lauren Develle, heard about the phone call, she decided to visit TyLon at his house in Jackson. When she arrived at TyLon's house, she assured him that thanks to his tip, the Grinch would not be stealing his Christmas this year. She then asked TyLon what he would do if he saw the Grinch. He said he'd call the police and have them come take him to jail.

Develle was so touched by this little boy that she ended up looking around for someone to play the Grinch. The next day, Office Lauren and TyLon escorted a man dressed up as the Grinch to a jail cell. The police chief Luke Thompson later told TyLon that when he turned 21, he could apply to be a real member of the police force (https://www.npr.org/2017/12/24/573072207/how-a-5-year-old-made-sure-the-grinch-didnt-steal-christmas-this-year).

Isn't that a great story? Tonight, I want us to lock up the Grinch inside all of us so he doesn't steal our joy this Christmas. The truth is, there is a Grinch in all of us. Too often, our bitterness and cynicism get in the way of enjoying Christmas.

We don't start off bitter and cynical. As children, Christmas was filled with wonder and delight. But something happens when we become adults. Life wears us out! It becomes exhausting.

When I was a kid playing with my dad, I used to always wonder why he got so tired and had to rest. I wanted to keep on playing. As a new father, now I know!

Life is so draining that Christmas can change from a season of joy to a season of numbing obligations. It can become another party to attend — another work deadline before Christmas. It may become another long trip to see relatives or another crazy relative to deal with. It may be the same routine with the same result — same, same, same.

One day I was walking in my neighborhood park. There is a great walking path that circles around the park. It goes right pass a jungle gym. As I was walking, I noticed a precious four-year-old boy, who goes to my church, playing on the jungle gym with his grandmother. I stopped to visit with them.

At first, the boy didn't recognize me. I had a hat and headphones on, listening to music. When he recognized me, he wanted to show me all that he could do on the jungle gym. So I watched. Then he came up to me and said, "I want to tell you a secret." I listened. I bent down and he whispered, "Do you have a girlfriend?" I said, "Sure, I do! She happens to be my wife."

I finished visiting and continued on my walk around the park with my headphones on. When I came back around to the jungle gym again I saw the young boy run up to me and say something. I didn't hear it because of my headphones. So I took them off and asked, "What was that?" He asked earnestly, "Are you going in circles? You were just here!" I said, "Son, you have no idea. Sometimes it does feel that way. Some days it does feel like I am going in circles."

Do you feel like you are going in circles? Does life seem like one exhausting event after the other? Do you feel like nothing ever changes? Allow our lesson from Titus to speak to you:

...we wait for the blessed hope — the appearing of the glory of our great God and Savior, Jesus Christ (Titus 2:13 NIV).

Many of us are desperately waiting for a hope that will renew and empower us. Tonight is all about experiencing the fruition of that very hope in Christ. This is the good news of Christmas. Jesus Christ has an incredible offer for us tonight. It's unlike any offer you'll ever receive. Jesus said:

"If you are tired from carrying heavy burdens, come to me and I will give you rest." (Matthew 11:28 CEV)

Rick Warren loves this verse because he believes many people don't expect God to say it. Instead, he wrote, they expect God to say,

"Come home to me, and I will give you rules. Come home to me, and I will give you regulations. Come home to me, and I will give you restrictions. Come home to me, and I will give you religion. Come home to me, and I will give you rituals." But God doesn't say any of those things. He says, *"Come home to me, and I will give you rest"* (https://www.oneplace.com/ministries/daily-hope/read/devotionals/daily-hope-with-rick-warren/come-home-to-gods-rest-daily-hope-with-rick-warren-december-22-2017-11784711.html).

Regardless of what you've heard, Christianity is not a

religion; it is a relationship. It is not something that confines you; it is something that sets you free. It is not something that shames you; it is something that empowers you.

I don't know how you think of God. I don't know what kind of religious upbringing you had. But one thing I do know is that God loves you and doesn't want to add more stress to your life. In fact, he wants to take stress away and give you love, hope, peace, and joy.

The reason why you're so tired and fatigued and stressed out all the time is because you're trying to live on your own power. God never meant for you to do that. God wants to give you the power you need. That's why the message of Christmas is not just about a birth; it is about a rebirth of life for those who come home to Jesus.

Anyone can experience this rebirth. All they have to do let go and stop trying to handle life on their own. All they have to do is come to Jesus.

Regardless of what you have done, regardless of where you have been, and regardless of how lost you may feel, you can come home to Jesus tonight and be reborn.

Even the Grinch was reborn by Christmas. Toward the end of the story, the Grinch was changed. Listen to the rest of the story:

> *And he puzzled three hours, till his puzzler was sore.*
> *Then the Grinch thought of something he hadn't before!*
> *"Maybe Christmas," he thought, "doesn't come from a store."*
> *"Maybe Christmas... perhaps... means a little bit more!"*
> (Dr. Seuss, *How the Grinch Stole Christmas*, Random House, 2013, Kindle Version).

Christmas does mean more — so much more. It is not just a birth. It is a rebirth! Come to Jesus and he will give you rest. He will give you life. He will give you joy. It's time for you to truly have a Merry Christmas. Come home to Jesus.

Amen.

Why The Cross?

Why did Jesus have to die a brutal death in order for God to forgive us? If you struggle with that question or you know someone who does, this message is for you.

Most Christians believe that the cross represents God's redemptive act in Christ forgiving us of sin and reconciling us to him. Take a look at these words from Hebrews:

> *For this reason he had to be made like them, fully human in every way, in order that he might become a merciful and faithful high priest in service to God, and that he might make atonement for the sins of the people. Because he himself suffered when he was tempted, he is able to help those who are being tempted* (Hebrews 2:17-18 NIV).

These verses are profound and mean a great deal to millions of Christians. However, the atonement is also what turns many people away from the Christian faith. A bloody cross is where many people get stuck.

I have a friend who is an agnostic. One time, he asked me, "Why are you Christians so obsessed with a bloody execution? It's macabre and disturbing. And if you are not talking about blood and guts, you are laying guilt trips on people. What do you get out of all that?"

Can you relate? Maybe you have friends who say something similar to you when you talk about church. Or maybe you are not a Christian and think, "That is why

I am not a Christian! I just don't get the whole sin and guilt thing. Why are Christians so bent on making people miserable? I also don't get the bloody cross. Why was that necessary for God to love us?"

Many people can accept Jesus as a great teacher, healer, and lover of sinners. Many people can take Jesus as the forgiver and encourager. And many people can take Jesus as the personification of God. But God needing blood, guts, and sacrifice to save us; to relieve his wrath and anger toward sin? Many folks can't go there. They can't believe in a God like that. Ever been there? Are you there now?

Many Christians struggle with what they have been told about the meaning of the cross. Perhaps it has been the one hurdle preventing you from following Christ. Perhaps you are a Christian, but it is still so difficult for you to accept what you have been told about the atonement. Maybe you like everything about the Christian faith but this particular idea of God needing a bloody execution in order to love and forgive.

Let me just name the elephant in the room: What so many people have a hard time with is called the "penal substitutionary theory of atonement." Basically, this understanding of the cross means that in order for a holy God to forgive sin, he required a blood sacrifice of a sinless person. So God sent his son as our substitute to get beat up and murdered so his wrath would be satisfied. After that, God's anger was relieved and he felt better about sin and forgave the world. This bloody execution made everything right for God. The shedding of innocent blood calmed God down. So, we sing about the blood of Jesus and how it makes us righteous.

Let me just say it for so many of you: What kind of a God is that? "I am a loving and forgiving God, but before I love and forgive you I need for my son to be brutally executed so my wrath for you will be relieved." As Benjamin Corey asks, "Why would God demand a blood sacrifice? Why does God need blood in order to forgive us? Why does the execution of an innocent person save the guilty? How does that work? Is there a better way to understand the cross?" In short, yes! (https://www.patheos.com/blogs/formerlyfundie/category/atonement/).

I don't believe in the kind of God that would demand a bloody sacrifice in order to forgive us. It's abuse! It's sadistic and cruel. It sounds like an ancient god of myth who needs a virgin thrown into a fire. It is not the God I know and love and the God who knows and loves me.

Now I know there are many who hold true to this idea of the cross. I'm okay with that. We can still love each other. But if what I have just said upsets you, please read the rest of this message before you decide to send me your email or letter.

What I am about to share may be a game changer for many of you. When you hear this message, you will truly understand the power of the cross. Some of you may finally decide to accept Christ as your Lord and Savior and follow him because of what I am about to tell you. Some of you are going to feel liberated about your faith for the first time in your life. Some of you are going to see the cross in a new way. Some of you are going to see God in a completely different way. This message may just change your life.

I want to thank Benjamin Corey for his ideas as I prepared this message. Corey is a very insightful theologian who has a blog on patheos.com. I encourage you to check it out. You may not agree with everything he writes, but he is worth reading. Most especially, his series on rethinking the atonement was helpful (https://www.patheos.com/blogs/formerlyfundie/category/atonement/).

Let's get to it: Why don't I believe that God needed a blood sacrifice in order to love and forgive us?

God did not like blood sacrifices.

Look at what David expressed in Psalm 51:16:

"You do not delight in sacrifice, or I would bring it; you do not take pleasure in burnt offerings."

Even though animal sacrifice was part of the law of Moses, it is clear that God was not wild about it. What did God desire?

For I desire mercy, not sacrifice, and acknowledgement of God rather than burnt offerings (Hosea 6:6 NIV).

Mercy. That's what God wanted. God also desired acknowledgement and for his people to put their faith in him. What's more, God was completely against human sacrifice. The Old Testament condemns human sacrifice multiple times (See Deuteronomy and Leviticus and Jeremiah 19:5 https://biblehub.com/jeremiah/19-5.htm).

The people of the Old Testament were reconciled to God.

You know all the heroes of the Old Testament? Abraham, Jacob, David, Moses, Gideon, Esther, Shadrach, Meshach, Abednego, and others? They were all justified by their faith -- and that was before the cross. We see this as early as Genesis 15:6:

Abram believed the LORD, and he credited it to him as righteousness (NIV).

Abraham and all the others were reconciled to God the same way that we are: by faith (https://www.patheos.com/blogs/formerlyfundie/if-jesus-had-to-die-before-we-could-be-forgiven-i-have-a-few-more-questions/).

A God desiring a human sacrifice is not the God revealed in Jesus Christ.

Let's start with Christmas. If God was bloodthirsty to calm his wrath, why didn't God just allow Herod to kill Jesus when he was born? Remember that when Jesus was born Herod felt threatened, and he sent the magi to find him so that he could kill him. If God was adamant about a blood sacrifice, why not take care of it in the beginning?

Now, let's look at the life of Jesus. As Christians, we believe in the incarnation of God. In other words, we believe Jesus was God in the flesh. If God hated sinners so much and needed a sacrifice in order for them to even be in his presence, then why did he hang out with sinners all the time? Sin should never be encouraged; but to say that God needed a blood sacrifice to be in the presence of sinners is ridiculous. When Jesus walked the earth, he preferred being with the worst in society.

If God cannot bear the presence of sin without the blood of Jesus, then the ministry of Jesus Christ has no meaning. God put skin on and walked with sinners, cared about them, and lovingly invited them to repent. More than that, if you read the gospels, you see Jesus forgiving people left and right. If God can't forgive us without Jesus' blood, then it makes no sense that Jesus willingly forgave people as a result of their faith. **This is what ticked off the religious people.** Take a look:

Jesus stepped into a boat, crossed over and came to his own town. Some men brought to him a paralyzed man, lying on a mat. When Jesus saw their faith, he said to the man, "Take heart, son; your sins are forgiven." At this, some of the teachers of the law said to themselves, "This fellow is blaspheming!" (Matthew 9:1-3 NIV).

I could bore you to tears with more details, but I think these last three points will suffice (https://www.patheos.com/blogs/formerlyfundie/if-jesus-had-to-die-before-we-could-be-forgiven-i-have-a-few-more-questions/).

So, all of this begs the big question: Why then did Jesus die on the cross? Why was that his ambition? Why did he go through with it? Why is the cross so important?

I answer those questions with one question that Corey asks: *What did Jesus actually say about his own death on the cross?* You see, that's what people miss when they talk about the cross. They debate and argue, but they never actually read what Jesus said about why he had to die. This is exactly where we find the answer — from the lips of Jesus. What Jesus has to say has the power to transform your understanding of the cross. More importantly, it has the power to transform your life.

In Matthew 20:28 and Mark 10:45, Jesus described his upcoming work on the cross in terms of giving his life... "as a ransom for many." (NIV). Corey reminds us that Jesus never described his upcoming death on the cross as a sacrifice to God. Just read the gospels. You will never find it. If Jesus had thought so, he would have said so. Instead, he used a very significant word, and I don't want you to miss it: "ransom." His death was the paying of a ransom (https://www.patheos.com/blogs/formerlyfundie/the-one-word-that-could-change-your-view-of-the-atonement/).

When a person is kidnapped, who are the people who demand a ransom? The bad guys, not the good guys! Ransoms are paid by the loved ones of the kidnapped. Ransoms are not demanded by those who are good but by those who are bad (https://www.patheos.com/blogs/formerlyfundie/the-one-word-that-could-change-your-view-of-the-atonement/).

So why was it Jesus' ultimate goal and ambition to die on the cross to pay a ransom for us? Who would be so cruel, twisted, sick, and demented enough to enjoy watching Jesus die a brutal death? Evil — that's right. Satan. He is the missing person in event of the cross. So here is a new way to understand the cross. Benjamin Corey puts it this way: "The cross was not a ransom demanded by God but paid by God" (https://www.patheos.com/blogs/formerlyfundie/the-one-word-that-could-change-your-view-of-the-atonement/).

We see this understanding of the cross in the very beginning of scripture in Genesis 3:15. When sin entered the world, take a look at what God says to the serpent when sin enters the world:

"He will crush your head, and you wll strike his heel" (Genesis 3:15 NIV).

This is a reference to Jesus' death on the cross! God is saying, "Yeah, you may hurt Jesus and kill him for a time, but you will be destroyed. Your head will be crushed!"

After Jesus' death and resurrection, we see it confirmed in the New Testament:

The reason the Son of God appeared was to destroy the devil's work (1 John 3:8 NIV).

What happened on the cross 2,000 years ago? Jesus faced the wrath of evil "head on," as Corey puts it, and defeated it with his transforming love. The only thing that could destroy the force of evil is the force of God's love. All the sin, hate, prejudice, death, and perversion that evil wanted to ruin this world with collided with the love and grace of God on our behalf on the cross -- and Jesus stopped it once and for all. Evil came at this world with everything it had and God in Christ stopped it in its tracks. When the cosmic bullet of evil came at us, Jesus jumped in front of us to save us. The cross was the climax of the cosmic war between God and evil -- and God's love in Christ won (https://www.patheos.com/blogs/formerlyfundie/the-one-word-that-could-change-your-view-of-the-atonement/).

Here is the message I want you understand: *The cross is not about satisfying the wrath of God but about the love of God overcoming the wrath of evil.* The cross means the love of God wins. The love of God is the most powerful force in the world. It is the one thing that changes everything. God defeated evil on the cross and everything that goes with it — death, fear, and hopelessness. So why is there still evil in the world? It is because evil is a sore loser! We are just cleaning up his mess. Everything evil, everything that goes against the force of God's love, will be mopped up and discarded when the kingdom of God comes in all of its glory.

One thing remains is the overcoming power of God's love revealed on the cross. This love is something that is available to each of us. It is available to you right now. Remember, the only thing that can stop the force of evil is the force of God's love. It is the one thing that changes everything.

Now that you have a different understanding of the cross, perhaps your heart is opening up to God's love. God's love is always available to you and can give you the power to overcome sin, hate, prejudice, pain, and anything else that is keeping you from wholeness in your life.

A colleague of mine told the story of a group of seminarians who played basketball together every week. They would always play in the same gym. There was a kind janitor who would wait patiently for them to finish their game so that he could lock up. One day, my colleague noticed the janitor reading the Bible as he waited. In fact, he was reading the book of Revelation, a book not even seminary students understand. My colleague approached the janitor and said, "I see you reading Revelation. Do you understand that book?" "Sure," he replied. "It's pretty easy to understand."

My colleague was intrigued. Revelation is a book that has confounded scholars and theologians, yet this man who never graduated high school understood it. So he asked the janitor, "Well, what does the book mean?" The janitor looked up at my colleague and said, "It means Jesus is gonna win!" (Stephen Grunlan, *Mixed Blessings,* Eugene, Oregon: Wipf and Stock Publishers, 2005, page 69).

You know what it means to be a Christian? It means letting Jesus be your hero. It means allowing his love to save you from all the things that are holding you back in life. It means allowing the power of his forgiveness to make you new. It means following him and reflecting his love in the world. Jesus already loves you. He has already forgiven you. He has already won the fight against evil. Just give yourself over to God's love and follow Jesus. Your life will never be the same. You will find all the things you have been longing for.

If you want Jesus to be your hero and desire to become a Christian, here is a prayer that may help you make that decision:

"Jesus, I want you to be my hero. I need your transforming love. I accept and receive your forgiveness of my sins. I open my heart to your grace and the power of your Spirit. Make me new. Make me whole. Guide me so my life may be a vessel of your love, that overcame the power of evil on the cross."

Amen.

We Believe In The Holy Spirit

In the middle of the Apostles Creed there are six critical words. The power of our faith is made possible because of these six words: "I believe in the Holy Spirit." Ephesians underscores the importance of the Holy Spirit:

> *When you believed, you were marked in him with a seal, the promised Holy Spirit, who is a deposit guaranteeing our inheritance until the redemption of those who are God's possession — to the praise of his glory* (Ephesians 1:13-14 NIV).

The Holy Spirit is the spirit of God that lives inside those who follow Christ. It was the Holy Spirit that motivated you to get out of bed on Sunday morning and go to worship. It is the Holy Spirit that inspires you to serve and love others. It is the Holy Spirit that guides you to make wise decisions. And it is the Holy Spirit who convicts you when you need to change. The Holy Spirit is God's very presence inside of you -- moving you, guiding you, and shaping you.

But how do we know when the Holy Spirit is guiding us? How are we supposed to know when we are being motivated by the Spirit and not something else? How do we know when it is God who is trying to speak to us and not another impulse inside us? There are a lot of voices inside and outside of us clamoring for our attention. How do we know which one is the Holy Spirit?

I remember studying John 10 with a group of youth. We got to the part when Jesus said, "The sheep follow him because they know his voice." This young man raised his hand and said, "Pastor, I pray to Jesus all the time but he never talks back. How am I supposed to know his voice when he never talks to me?"

Have you ever wondered what the Holy Spirit's voice sounds like? James Earl Jones? Alexa of Google? Or does it sound more like the woman's voice on your smartphone GPS system?

The truth is, if we are literally hearing audible voices, we probably need to take a trip to the psychiatrist, not the sanctuary. I am not saying it's impossible to hear an audible voice, but God doesn't usually operate like that. Instead, God, through the Holy Spirit, speaks to us through passion, desire, instinct, conviction, and circumstance. To say we are hearing the Spirit's voice means we are being moved by the Spirit in some way.

But, again, how are we supposed to know we are being moved by the Holy Spirit? There have been times in my life when I have been faced with a decision or have desired guidance. When I made my decision or chose my path, I thought I was being guided by the Spirit -- but I was not. The whole thing blew up in my face. I prayed about it; read scripture. I felt great about it. I did all the right things -- but it became clear I had made the wrong decision. I thought, "What did I miss? Where did I go wrong?"

Ever been there? Ever been confident that the decision you made was the right one; the one the Spirit was guiding you to make -- and then disaster hit, and all signs pointed to your having made a bad decision?

Maybe you are faced with a decision today and you need some kind of guidance. You're seeking some sign of the Spirit, some nudge in the right direction -- but you are not really sure how you will know when it is the Holy Spirit guiding you. Or maybe you have made a decision and you want evidence from God that it was the right decision, but you don't know what to look for.

I am going to reveal how you can be sure 99% of the time that the Holy Spirit is guiding you. I am going to show how you can be sure whether or not the decision that you made was the right one. I am going to show you how you can confidently know you are being moved by the Holy Spirit.

I discovered something huge along my journey about how the Holy Spirit works. Through trial and error, reading scripture, and listening to wise counsel I learned the key to knowing when I am going in the direction of the Holy Spirit. This key has helped me avoid a lot of mistakes. Learning this key will help you avoid a lot of mistakes too! More importantly it will help you find God's path for you.

To help us discover this key, I want us to take a look at something Jesus said to his disciples about the Holy Spirit. These words appear in the fourteenth chapter of John. Jesus is comforting his disciples in the Upper Room. They know something bad is going to happen. Jesus is trying to break the news to them that he is going away and he is trying to encourage them. Jesus says something in the midst of his comforting sermon that I think is one of the most outrageous things he ever said. Take a look:

"Very truly I tell you, whoever believes in me will do the works I have been doing, and they will do even greater things than these, because I am going to the Father" (John 14:12 NIV).

67

The first time I saw that, I thought, "Whoa! Do greater works than Jesus? What is he talking about? Jesus healed the sick, walked on water, made the blind see, and raised the dead! How in the world can any of us do greater works than Jesus?"

Even more confusing are these words: "Because I am going to the Father." I am sure the disciples were thinking the same thing that I was thinking: "Wait, don't we need Jesus to do all of these amazing things? How can we do great things if he is leaving us? That doesn't make any sense." Jesus brings some clarity by saying:

> "If you love me, keep my commands. And I will ask the Father, and he will give you another advocate to help you and be with you forever—the Spirit of truth..." (John 14:15-17 NIV).

Here, Jesus is introducing the Holy Spirit. This is when the light bulb went on for me. We are able to do greater works than Jesus because when Jesus ascended to the Father, his Spirit began to live in each of his followers. This means Jesus' power and influence multiplied and multiplied throughout the earth. So, when you look at and compare all the work the church has done over the last 2,000 years to Jesus' three-year earthly ministry, it is much greater.

Jesus uses some interesting words to describe the Holy Spirit. Jesus calls it an "advocate." The Greek word was used to describe a witness who was called in to support your case in a court of law. Or it could also be used to describe a lawyer who pleads your case when you have been charged with a serious crime. An advocate was also used to describe someone who motivated athletes who were discouraged or fatigued. Jesus also referred to the

Holy Spirit as the "Spirit of Truth" because the Spirit guides us into truth and reminds us what Jesus taught. Later, Jesus described the Spirit like spring water that flows within us.

But how are we supposed to know that what is bubbling up inside of us is the Holy Spirit and not something else? How do we recognize the Spirit when we need to make decisions, find wisdom, or be guided through difficulty? Well take a look at what Jesus says next:

> "— *the Spirit of truth. The world cannot accept him, because it neither sees him nor knows him. But you know him, for he lives with you and will be in you"* (John 14:17 NIV).

Jesus is saying that the world -- those who live as if there was no God -- can't recognize the Spirit because they interpret everything that happens out of their own ability. But Jesus' followers know him because he will be with them and in them. In other words, the difference between us and the world is that we see things based on what God is able to do through us.

So we recognize the Holy Spirit's work by its ability, not our own. When I made this conclusion, these words from Jesus just a few verses later popped out at me:

> *"Apart from me you can do nothing"* (John 15:5 NIV).

So here is what I figured out:

When you find ability beyond you, the Spirit is with you.

This is the key to being sure the Spirit is moving in your life. This is the key to knowing when the Holy Spirit is guiding you. When you find power beyond you, the Spirit is with you. When you find wisdom beyond you, the Spirit is with you. When you know you could not have accomplished something on your own, you can be sure it was the Holy Spirit. When you have been led to a place you would have never found on your own, you can be sure it was the Holy Spirit. When you found strength to do something that seemed impossible, you can be sure it was the Holy Spirit. When you are attempting to do something that requires God's help to get it done, you can be sure you are in the right place!

I see the Spirit's work like being on a swing as a child. Do you remember that? I do. I could not wait to get to the park to swing on the swing set. I loved to go really high. But as a kid, I would sit on the swing and try to get the swing moving on my own -- but couldn't. So I would call out to my mom or dad, "Can you give me a push?" My mom would show up and gently push me back and forth and get me going. However, when my dad showed up, he knew I liked to go really high so he would pull me up high and let me go! I needed the push or the big pull to get me going and to reach the heights to which I wanted to go.

The Holy Spirit works like that. Sometimes, it is a nudge; and sometimes, the Holy Spirit pulls us way up and lets us go. But one thing is always the same: It is the power of the Spirit that enables us to swing high and fly. Many Christians are not operating on full power because they are not relying on the Holy Spirit. The Spirit does not force itself on us. We have to be open to it. We have to call out, "Holy Spirit, I need help. I need a push."

I remember mowing the lawn as a kid growing up in Atlanta. We had a big front yard and back yard. The back yard had a big hill. It was hard work. I remember my dad buying a new Toro lawn mower for me. "Thanks, Dad — how thrilling!" He said it was supposed to make it easier to mow. Well, that thing was heavy. It was twice the size as the old one and twice as difficult to move. I kept wondering why my dad thought it would make it easier to mow. I was breaking my back trying to move the thing.

One day, my dad saw me struggling with the mower. He came up to me and said, "Charley, don't you know this thing has motorized wheels?" I replied, "No, dad! Thanks for telling me!" He showed me that all I had to do was pull down a lever below the handle bar and pull it back up -- and that thing would almost mow by itself. You could even control the speed and everything. I don't know how I missed it originally, but when I activated those wheels, it felt like an easy stroll through my yard. When you find ability beyond you, the Spirit is with you.

This may be the missing piece in your life as a Christian. Maybe you are not finding the strength or wisdom you seek because you have not activated the Holy Spirit that lives within you. Every follower of Christ has the Spirit of God within them. John Wesley believed that even nonbelievers have the Spirit of God inside them but that it lies dormant. We must give the Holy Spirit permission to work. When was the last time you activated the Spirit within you? What are you attempting right now that only the Holy Spirit could accomplish through you? What are you doing right now that you know would lead to utter failure without God? If we are not living our faith in this way, we are missing out on one of the great joys of being a follower of Christ.

The church needs this message too. If the church is not relying on the Holy Spirit, we are not a church. We are an entertainment center or just another charity -- but we are not a church. Being open to the movement of the Spirit is essential to being a healthy and thriving church. A church can survive for a time on a good band or choir, a motivational speaker, and a Facebook page -- but without the work of the Holy Spirit, a church cannot sustain itself. It cannot be the vessel God calls it to be. Charles Spurgeon said, "Without the Spirit of God, we can do nothing. We are as ships without the wind; branches without sap -- and like coals without fire, we are useless."

Unfortunately, too many churches try to do ministry without the aid of the Holy Spirit. Then they wonder why they never grow. We have become real good at putting a governor on the Spirit of God. We have become rather skilled at stifling the Spirit when it doesn't line up with our whims and fancies or when it threatens to inconvenience us. The Spirit is strong -- but it doesn't force itself on anyone or any church -- so it will go only as far as we allow it.

I know of a pastor who didn't like the direction the church was going. He felt it didn't have much life. It wasn't doing the things that a church ought to be doing. It wasn't praying enough or serving enough. It wasn't studying the Bible enough. So he, led by the Spirit, started all of these small groups in the church. Lo and behold, they started to catch on, got all fired up, and started to change things and shake things up. And the leader of this crew started to speak all across town. He lifted up the gospel, and all these people listened to him and responded. They received Christ. He was the talk of the town. His church was none too pleased with all this excitement and exuberance; with all this change. They got annoyed with this group in the church and with their leader. So, what did the church do? They wouldn't allow him to speak in worship anymore. His name? John Wesley. The group? Methodists!

The Spirit was alive and well in Wesley, which is why the church rejected him and his ministry. Thank God the Spirit prevailed! If not, we would not be here. But imagine how many Spirit-driven movements have died because the church closed its doors to the Holy Spirit.

In 1983, Australia threatened to take the America's Cup from the United States. The United States had won the prestigious yacht racing cup for years -- but that year Australia was a force to be reckoned with. Australia and the United States were tied, with one race to go. The day came for the final race. Scores of people came to watch the race. Television cameras from all over the world were there. The boats were ready. The crews were ready. The yachts pulled into place at the starting line. All was ready -- but there was no race. Why? There was no wind. "In yachting, no wind means no race" (Eddie Fox and George Morrie, *Faith Sharing*, Nashville: Discipleship Resources, 1996, pages 113 and 114).

It's true. Nothing happens without the wind. Did you know that in the Bible the Hebrew and Greek words for Spirit literally mean "wind"? Jesus said it is like a mystery, the wind. You don't see the wind, and yet you know when it comes and when it goes. It was the wind of the Spirit that blew through the early church and spread the gospel like wildfire.

Are you looking for the wind of the Spirit in your life? Pray:

"Lord, help me to see the evidence of you at work in my life and where it is pointing me. Open my eyes to see your hand in my life. May I sense where you are working beyond me and trust that is where you are guiding me."

"When you find ability beyond you, the Spirit is with you."

I used to love looking at this big palm tree on a golf course. Every time I passed it, I would admire it. Then one day, when I passed it, I found that it had fallen to the ground. I was upset and said, "I wonder what caused that?" And someone said, "The wind."

I once knew a man who hated the church. He told everybody he didn't believe in God. He said that religion was for weak people who couldn't stand on their own two feet. Then one day, all that hardness crumbled to the ground. His heart was changed. He started going to church and he never stopped going. I don't know what happened! Someone said, "It's the wind."

There I was, sixteen years old, minding my own business. I was playing tennis, having crushes on girls, telling jokes, and having fun. I was sitting in church with my parents and sisters. We were passing the mints, playing tic-tac-toe, and writing notes about where we wanted to go to lunch. Then this man got up to preach. I had never heard anyone like him before. I was inspired. Next thing I know, I am shaking his hand at the back door of the church, telling him I want to be a preacher! Me, a preacher? What happened? What caused that? You know what I think it was? The wind.

I had just gotten home from a long Sunday morning at the church. My wife Brandy handed me a pregnancy test and it read positive. What? We were told we could never have children. For eighteen years we were told it wasn't going to happen. I almost fell to the floor. I wondered how? Then it dawned on me — it was the wind. My son Paul was not conceived by the Holy Spirit. I certainly played a role! But I can tell you this: We could not have done it without the wind -- the Holy Spirit.

When you find ability beyond you, the Spirit is with you.

Amen.

*(Portions of this sermon were adapted from my sermon "The Wind" in my book from CSS, *Mission Possible.*)

The Most Important Question

Have you ever heard a golfer miss a three-foot putt and say, "Thomas Jefferson!?" What about a plumber mash his thumb and scream, "Robert E. Lee!?" I haven't either, but many shout the name of a man who was born two thousand years ago in a backwoods town to a poor unwed teenage mother. Many exclaim the name of a man who was shamefully executed as a criminal at the age of thirty and died homeless and poor. Ironic, isn't it?

For some mysterious reason, Jesus is the most famous figure in all of history. More songs have been written about him, more artwork has been created of him, and more books have been written about him than of any other person who ever lived. In fact, Jesus of Nazareth had such an influence on human history that we measure time by him. Our calendar is divided into the years before and after his birth — BC and AD.

For years, *Time* magazine has named a "Person of The Year" on its January cover. In 2013, the editors of *Time* decided to go for the doozie and name the most significant person in history. They did an exhaustive study and a complex analysis of historical figures. Guess who won? *Jesus* (Rick Lawrence, *The Jesus-Centered Life*, Group Publishing, 2016, Kindle version).

Yet, do we really know who Jesus was? Do we really know? I remember the first time I saw a picture of Jesus. I was just a little boy in Sunday school drinking grape

Kool Aid® and eating graham crackers. On the wall of the classroom was a sweet picture of Jesus with children all around him. He was smiling and looked like the nicest man in the universe. He looked like a divine Mister Rogers. He taught us to be kind to one another and to love everyone. I was comforted by the picture.

Yet, as I got older I began to wonder: Why would a man who taught others to be kind to one another get brutally executed? Who could bring themselves to crucify Mister Rogers?

Whenever my Sunday school teachers talked about Jesus, they would also teach about being careful of the people you hang out with. They would talk about respecting those in authority. Yet Jesus befriended social misfits and outcasts. He hung out with people most of us would not be caught dead with. He was accused by the religious establishment of being a party animal and of hanging out with riff raff. Jesus is usually associated with people who follow the rules and play it safe, yet he didn't do either!

Many of us believe in Jesus, but what do we believe about him -- and why should it make any difference to the way we live our lives today? What difference should it make that a man lived 2,000 years ago in a place called Galilee? Can't we see him as just a great teacher and significant figure of history -- and be on our way? Or should he mean more than that? Well, according to the gospel writers and 2,000 years of Christian history and tradition, Jesus should make all the difference in the world. In the tenth chapter of Acts, we are reminded of the importance of Jesus and the appropriate response to what he accomplished on earth:

"You know what has happened throughout the province of Judea, beginning in Galilee after the baptism that John preached — how God anointed Jesus of Nazareth with the

Holy Spirit and power, and how he went around doing good and healing all who were under the power of the devil, because God was with him."

'We are witnesses of everything he did in the country of the Jews and in Jerusalem. They killed him by hanging him on a cross, but God raised him from the dead on the third day and caused him to be seen. He was not seen by all the people, but by witnesses whom God had already chosen — by us who ate and drank with him after he rose from the dead. He commanded us to preach to the people and to testify that he is the one whom God appointed as judge of the living and the dead. All the prophets testify about him that everyone who believes in him receives forgiveness of sins through his name.' (Acts 10:37-43 NIV).

When you really study Jesus -- who he was, what he taught, and what he did -- you are faced with a question — a very profound and penetrating question. And how you answer this question will determine your destiny as a human being. Your answer to this question will determine how you live, work, and relate to the people you love and the people you hate. Your answer to this question will determine the direction and quality of your life. Your answer to this question will determine whether or not your life counts for something. Your answer to this question will determine the way you see yourself, others, and the world.

To get to this question, I want us to take a hard look at what Jesus said about himself. If we want to get to the real truth about Jesus, it would be a good idea to move away for a moment from what history and culture say about him and instead look at what he said about himself.

In John 10:30-33, Jesus makes an astonishing claim:

> *"The Father and I are one." The Jews took up stones again to stone him. Jesus replied, "I have shown you many good works from the Father. For which of these are you going to stone me?" The Jews answered, "It is not for a good work that we are going to stone you, but for blasphemy, because you, though only a human being, are making yourself God"*(John 10:30-33 NRSV).

Over and over again, *Jesus claimed he was God*. No other religious figure in history claimed this. Buddha, Krishna, Gandhi, and Mohammed never made this claim. Only Jesus did. Any person who makes such a claim is either nuts or telling the truth.

Let's look at another astonishing claim of Jesus in Luke 5:20-21:

> *When he saw their faith, he said, "Friend, your sins are forgiven you." Then the scribes and the Pharisees began to question, "Who is this who is speaking blasphemies? Who can forgive sins but God alone?"*(Luke 5:20-21 NRSV).

We also see that *Jesus claimed to forgive sins*. He claimed to have the power to wipe away all those things in life that put us in the dark; those things that make us bitter and render us unable to experience joy. He claimed to have the power to set us free from those things in life that enslave us.

Have you ever wanted a second chance? Have you ever wanted a new beginning? Jesus claimed to have the power to give you a fresh start.

Let's look at another astonishing claim from Jesus. Most of you know this one by heart John 3:16:

For God so loved the world that he gave his only Son, so that everyone who believes in him may not perish but may have eternal life (John 3:16 NRSV).

Jesus claimed that if put our trust in him, *he will give us eternal life* — a quality of life with God that begins now and is eternal in its duration! Jesus claimed that he could give us power over death! Jesus claimed that he could give us power to live forever with him.

Have you ever feared death? Have you ever wondered what is on the other side? Have you ever longed to live in a world that has been healed? Have you ever yearned to have a body that is no longer in pain? Jesus claimed that if we follow him, we don't have to fear death. It is simply the threshold to a glorious life with him forever.

Jesus claimed to be God, to forgive sins, and to give us eternal life. When we truly see who Jesus claimed he was, we are forced to make a decision about him. The life of Jesus demands a response. You can't read about the life of Jesus and simply say he was a great teacher or a notable figure in history. That choice is not on the table. Anyone who made these three huge claims is either a lunatic or is telling the truth. So, the pivotal question for each one of us is, "Who Jesus is to you?" -- not who Jesus is to your grandmother, mother, father, or friends, but who Jesus is to you? Is he insane or is he God? Is he crazy or is he the Savior? Is he nuts or is he Lord of lords? Those are the only two choices we have.

Who is Jesus to you? How you answer that question will determine your destiny, your choices, your purpose, the quality of your life and relationships, your joy, and how you view death and dying. You see, the question is personal. It is *very* personal. It's about whether or not you want a relationship with Jesus that will strengthen, encourage, and sustain you the rest of your life.

81

Maybe you are thinking, "I believe in God." That is not enough. What kind of God do you believe in? We must define and know the character of the God we believe in. Colossians says that "Christ is the image of the invisible God." John 1:14 proclaims, "And the Word became flesh and dwelt among us." (NKJV).Only the Christian faith makes that claim about God — God became one of us to save us and to be in relationship with us. On our own, we could never understand who God is. On our own, we could never save ourselves. This is why God came to us in Jesus. This is why we believe in Jesus Christ.

Several years ago, I recall taking our dog out before going to bed. As I was waiting for her on our screened-in porch, I heard a flutter behind me. When I turned around, I couldn't believe what I saw. There, perched on one of our patio chairs, was a screech owl. Its big eyes were just staring at me. It was a beautiful creature. I wondered what it was doing on my porch. Soon it dawned on me that the poor thing could not find its way out. The whole porch is screened in, and only one of the doors is left open to the backyard. It was clear that it had flown in through that open door but that it could not find that open door again to get out.

The first thing I did was open the front porch door so two doors would be open, and I foolishly pointed to both of them as if the owl understood human behavior. The owl just kept looking at me with those big eyes. The next thing I did was walk outside both of the doors and attempt to wave the owl out; "Come on; come on!" The owl continued to stare at me. Then I remembered that the porch lights were not on, so I turned them on, and the owl just stared at me. Suddenly, another owl swooped down just outside the porch, wanting to free its friend and bring it home -- but it couldn't find its way into the porch.

I finally gave up. As I was walking up the stairs to bed, I thought, "Now, this will preach! The only way I could free that owl and bring it home is to become an owl myself." Isn't that what God has done for us at Christmas? God has become one of us to show us the way home.

(If you are still wondering about the owl, the next morning the owl was gone.)

We must remember what Peter Kreeft told his class at Boston University: "Christ changed every human being he ever met. If people claim to have met Jesus without being changed, they have not met Jesus. When you touch Jesus, you touch lightning."

Perhaps you feel your heart being opened today. You have tried everything else life has to offer and it has never satisfied. You've been there, done that, and have thrown away the T-shirt! Maybe you are ready to put your hope in Christ.

Rick Lawrence is a Christian ministry guru. He has written bestselling books and travels the globe leading conferences, seminars, and workshops on how to grow churches and do ministry effectively. In his book The Jesus - Centered Life Lawrence wrote about a day when he was leading a workshop for ministry leaders and pastors. He felt depressed and worn out. The material and techniques he usually covered were not exciting to him anymore. He decided to throw away his notes and ask those in the workshop to talk about how Jesus was active in their lives. He said that for the next two hours, the room was electric with the presence of Jesus. He had never felt more passionate about a workshop before.

After the workshop, Lawrence attended other workshops and became depressed again. He felt terrible and could not put his finger on it. He found a big comfy chair in the middle of the conference arena; and as he sat there watching people walk by with their notes, books, and resources, he prayed, "Lord Jesus, why do I feel this way? Why do I feel so terrible?" Lawrence said that he heard Jesus' voice almost audibly reply, "Because you are bored with everything but me now" (Rick Lawrence, "The Jesus-Centered Life," Group Publishing, 2016, Kindle version).

There are not enough golf courses, football games, and trips to the lake that can give you what Jesus Christ can give you. Only Jesus can truly satisfy and bring you home. So, who is Jesus to you? Your answer will make all the difference to your life.

Amen.

Thankful Living In A Grumpy World

The apostle Paul was one grateful person. I am sure this is one of the reasons why he was effective in his ministry. He had an "attitude of gratitude." Like many of his letters, Paul began his letter to the Corinthians this way:

> *I always thank my God for you because of his grace given you in Christ Jesus* (1 Corinthians 1:4 NIV).

Not only does Paul continually give thanks in his letters, but many times in scripture he strongly encourages us to do the same:

> *In everything give thanks: for this is the will of God in Christ Jesus concerning you* (1 Thessalonians 5:18 KJV).

One of the reasons we come to worship is to give thanks. As we sing hymns and say prayers, we are giving thanks to God. Why? Not only because God is worthy of our thanksgiving and worship because there is healing power in gratitude. There is substantial medical evidence that suggests that a sense of gratitude is critical to a healthy life. Gratitude can make all the difference in the world. It can transform us and our relationships. There is power in gratitude.

I saw the power of gratitude firsthand while eating in a mall food court several years ago. It was during the Christmas holiday season. The area was packed with people. It took a while to find a table. When I sat down to eat my meal, I noticed a family sitting next to me. They had just sat down to eat as well. They asked their young daughter, maybe four years old, to say the blessing -- and she prayed for everything but the kitchen sink. She prayed for Santa and Rudolph. She prayed for her parents, the weather, and her dog. She covered everything. As she prayed, something interesting happened. It got very quiet in our section of tables. When she finished her prayer, people had smiles on their faces. For a moment, the stress of the holidays had been replaced with gratitude.

That little girl's prayer changed our mood. I think everyone sitting near that child felt more grateful not only for the food in front of us but also for the blessings around us. We had peace and joy in our hearts.

If only we could feel that way more often. We live in a grumpy, selfish world. It is so easy to get caught up in ourselves and what we don't have. It's so easy to get irritated over what people do or don't do. And it's so easy to get discouraged over what doesn't work out.

Maybe that is where you are today. You struggle with having an attitude of gratitude and you want that to change. You want to be more at peace with life and experience more joy and thanksgiving.

How can we capture the peace and joy of gratitude more often in our lives? Well we can go back to scripture. Once again, the apostle Paul shows us exactly how to experience more joy through gratitude. In the first chapter of Philippians, Paul gives us the key:

"I thank my God every time I remember you. In all my prayers for all of you, I always pray with joy because of your partnership in the gospel from the first day until now" (Philippians 1:3-5).

Paul is expressing his gratitude for all the special people in his life and ministry. As he remembered his friends, he was filled with gratitude -- and that gratitude led him to pray a prayer of joyful thanksgiving to God. By his example, Paul shows us how to experience gratitude in our hearts. If you struggle with feeling grateful, just take a moment to remember your blessings. You'll discover rather quickly there is much to be thankful for. For example, you can begin today by remembering what you have.

Remember What You Have

What would your life be like without your blessings? Kent Crockett, in his book *I Once Was Blind, But Now I Squint*, tells about his father who had to undergo radiation treatments for throat cancer. King Duncan commented on the book, saying,

> *The therapy damaged his taste buds so that he couldn't taste food. His inability to enjoy a meal made eating a dreaded duty. The doctors told him his taste might return after the treatments were finished, but no one could say for certain.*
> *Weeks passed, then months. Every meal became a forced feeding to keep him alive. After eating flavorless food for over a year, he sat down for dinner one evening. Reluctantly, he forced the fork inside his mouth and discovered that his taste had returned. What most people would call a bland dinner had become the best meal he had eaten in his life.*

Through losing his taste and then regaining it, [his] father learned to relish each morsel as never before. He became thankful for the ability to taste because he now had a reference point. He would never forget what it was like to eat tasteless food.

"You don't have to lose something in order to be thankful,' says Crockett. *'You can develop a taste for your blessings by simply realizing what life would be like without them"* (King Duncan, "Gratitude: A Matter of Perspective" https://sermons.com/sermon/gratitude-a-matter-of-perspective/1483503).

Think about some of the blessings you enjoy. Imagine you lost those blessings. Now imagine you found them. Just think how grateful you would be!

Someone said that "Christians are people who do not have to consult their bank account to see how wealthy they are."

Do you want to feel thankful? Remember what you have. But I also encourage you to remember who you have.

Remember Who You Have

What would your life be like without the people you love? Brett Blair writes, "In the book *A Window on the Mountain*," Winston Pierce told of his high school class reunion. A group of the old classmates were reminiscing about things and people they were grateful for. One man mentioned that he was particularly thankful for Mrs. Wendt, for she was a special teacher who had taught him not only school lessons but also lessons about life. Acting on a suggestion, the man wrote a letter of appreciation to Mrs. Wendt and addressed it to the high school. The note was forwarded and eventually found the old teacher."

"About a month later, the man received a response. It was written in feeble handwriting and read as follows:

> *My dear Willie, I can't tell you how much your letter meant to me. I am now in my nineties, living alone in a small room, cooking my own meals, and feeling very lonely. You will be interested to know that I taught school for forty years and yours is the first letter of appreciation I ever received. It came on a blue, cold morning and it cheered me as nothing has for years. Willie, you have made my day* (Brett Blair, "Giving Thanks Before Thanksgiving" — https://sermons.com/sermon/giving-thanks-before-thanksgiving/1340730.

Remember the special people in your life. Take time to write them a note or to give them a call. This will help you feel the power of gratitude. Most of all, the best way to experience the power of gratitude is to remember who has you.

Remember Who Has You

A popular Thanksgiving tradition for many people is to go around the table and name a few things they are thankful for. I think it is a great tradition, but I like the one Brett Blair recommends. Instead of naming what you are thankful for, go around the table and have each person answer this statement: "If it had not been for God...."

Think about it. Where would you be right now without God? Empty? Without purpose? Lost? Reflect on God's faithfulness to you this year and express it to those you love.

I also encourage you to write down what you share about God's faithfulness. Writing down the ways you are thankful to God can be a powerful resource down the road. If you ever get lost in life, just take out what you have written about God's faithfulness to you -- and it will encourage you.

One of my favorite movies is *The Blind Side*. It's based on a true story about an abandoned homeless high school kid called "Big Mike." He gets taken in by a loving family, and they become his legal guardians. They nurture him so he can live out his dream of playing professional football.

There is a powerful scene in the movie that takes place on Thanksgiving Day. It's just a day or two after Big Mike is taken in by this family. In the kitchen sits a mountain of food that has been prepared. Mike can't believe all the food that is before him, but the family just takes it for granted. They grab all they can and run back to the sofa with filled plates to watch the big game. Mike humbly takes a bit of food and puts it on his plate and then walks in another direction. The camera slowly moves away from the family on the sofa stuffing their faces to the big empty dining room table. There is Big Mike, sitting in the dining room table all by himself. He never had a big dining room table to sit around. The mom, played by Sandra Bullock, notices Big Mike sitting by himself. She immediately turns off the television and orders the family to go into the dining room to eat. They set the table with silverware, china, and candles. They all sit around Big Mike, hold hands, and thank God for all of their many blessings. Big Mike reminded them just how blessed they were.

If you remember what you have, remember who you have, and remember who has you, you will always be filled with gratitude.

Amen.

Epiphany 3
1 Corinthians 1:10-18

Dealing With Difficult People

How do you deal with difficult people? By difficult, I mean all categories — the gossips, the bullies, the manipulators, the intimidators, the blamers, the criticizers, the complainers, the whiners, and more. Just fill in the blank. Do you know anyone that fits into one of those categories? I imagine you do. This message is going to help you handle difficult people with biblical wisdom.

You might be surprised to know that the early church was filled with difficult people. In fact, much of the content of Paul's letters addressed dissension and dysfunctional behavior in the church. Take a look:

I appeal to you, brothers and sisters, in the name of our Lord Jesus Christ, that all of you agree with one another in what you say and that there be no divisions among you, but that you be perfectly united in mind and thought (1 Corinthians 1:10 NIV).

We can only imagine the situation within the Corinthian church that had prompted those words from Paul. But we can be sure it involved some difficult people!

I can appreciate Paul's efforts in calling the church to get along. I must confess that being a pastor is not all robes, Bibles, leather chairs, and the Hallelujah Chorus. When you are a spiritual leader for a large community of faith, you are going to have to deal with some difficult people.

I have had to deal with some real doozies! The problem is that there was no class in seminary on how to deal with difficult people. Along the way, I have made mistakes -- and, through those mistakes, I have gained some life-changing wisdom about dealing with difficult people.

I have a hunch you would like to hear this wisdom I have learned. Perhaps you are tired of listening to that overbearing family member who belittles everyone. Maybe you work with someone in the office who gossips about everyone -- and he is driving you crazy. Maybe you have an in-law who criticizes everything you do. No matter what you do, it is never good enough! Perhaps you have a neighbor or friend that you see from time to time who talks behind your back and seems to sabotage you. Worst of all, you might live with folks who are always blaming you or someone else for their problems, and they never take responsibility for themselves.

What do you do with people like that? Is there a way to respond to difficult people that you won't live to regret? Is there an effective way to respond to difficult people that won't get you fired, ruin your own reputation, or get you arrested? Is there a way to deal with difficult people that will not compromise your faith?

There was a time in my life when I was struggling with a difficult person and I was asking those same questions. At that time, I came across a passage of scripture that changed everything for me. The passage liberated me and enabled me to respond to difficult people effectively and appropriately. But not only that! The new insight I gained actually helps me receive a blessing whenever I deal with difficult people. That's right. This passage helps me receive a blessing when I deal with difficult people.

I want to share this passage because I believe if you apply the wisdom of the text, you can also be liberated and receive a blessing when dealing with difficult people. The text can be found in 1 Peter chapter 3. 1 Peter is a great book to read when dealing with difficult people because it was written to persecuted Christians who were being pounced on by all kinds of difficult people. Christians had been thrown out of Jerusalem and were spread out all over Asia Minor, and they were being persecuted by the Roman government. These Christians claimed Jesus as Lord -- while, for the Romans, only Caesar was Lord. So the writer of 1 Peter shares how they should respond to those who are against them.

1 Peter 3:9a says: *Do not repay evil for evil or abuse for abuse; but on the contrary, repay with a blessing.*(NRSV) Wow! This was an epic idea then and it is an epic idea today. When these words were written, it was lawful to retaliate; to get even with someone who went against you. Today, that seems like acceptable behavior too. Yet 1 Peter basically says, "As followers of Christ, that is not an option for you. We don't retaliate. In fact, we go one step further. We respond to insults and evil with goodness and love."

1 Peter 3:9b says: *It is for this that you were called—that you might inherit a blessing.*(NRSV) So as followers of Christ, we are *called* to respond this way — to respond to evil with goodness. It is not a suggestion, or an idea, or an option. It is a command from Christ. We are calledto this! But if the idea seems difficult or impossible, you need to know you will receive a blessing by responding this way. What is the blessing? Let's keep reading.

Read 1 Peter 3:10-11. The writer of 1 Peter was quoting a psalm there. It seems like a tall task to always seek peace, especially when you are faced with a difficult person.

When you are faced with that difficult person who is driving you up the wall, seeking peace is the last thing on your mind! How can you do it? Well, look at 1 Peter says next.

1 Peter 3:12a says: *For the eyes of the Lord are on the righteous and his ears are attentive to their prayer* (NIV). How do we repay evil with a blessing? By understanding that God is watching us, cheering for us, pulling for us, and sending power to us. How? Through prayer! God is attentive to our prayers. Now, there is a concept! Have you prayed for a person who is difficult? Have you ever prayed for God to help you with a person who is difficult? It works! Let's keep reading.

1 Peter 3:14b-15 says: *Do not be intimidated, but in your hearts sanctify Christ as Lord* (NRSV). 1 Peter reinforces the fact that we do not act on our own power. We should not be afraid or intimidated by difficult people. When we allow our hearts to draw closer to Christ and his love, he will give us the power to respond to insult with a blessing.

Read 1 Peter 3:15-16. These verses are amazing. When we choose to respond to evil with a blessing, it is going to turn heads. It is going to get attention -- because no one acts this way. In fact, it may embarrass the difficult person. When we rise above the crowd and respond to insults and criticism with love and goodness, people are going to notice -- and there is a good chance they are going to wonder what is different about us. So, we must be prepared to tell them why we act the way we do. So, what do we tell them? 1 Peter tells us in verse 18.

1 Peter 3:18 says: *For Christ also suffered for sins once for all, the righteous for the unrighteous, in order to bring you to God* (NRSV). This is what you tell them. For, you see, all of us can be difficult. All of us can be abrasive and insensitive. All of us can be impossible to deal with. And how did

Christ respond to us? With unbelievable love, grace, and mercy! We repay evil and insults with a blessing because that is what Christ has done for us. So often we forget this. When we are dealing with a difficult person, we forget we can be difficult too. We are not as hard on ourselves as we are on others. But as we draw closer to Christ and his love we remember what Christ has done for us.

Here is the message: *We are never more like Christ than when we love the unlovely.* We are never more like Christ than when we respond to evil with goodness — when we return insult with a blessing. Your response to difficult people will either betray your faith in Christ or reveal it. Responding to difficult people is perhaps your greatest opportunity to witness to the power of God's love in Jesus Christ. If you don't respond the right way, you may miss the best opportunity to share the love of Christ. Your life is your message. How you respond to difficult people is your sermon!

So, let me get down to how this works. Soon, you may have to be around someone who is very difficult. Here is what you do:

Pray persistently. Today, start praying for that person and ask God to help you respond in a loving manner. It is amazing what can happen when we pray for difficult people. God will help us. Praying for a difficult people also helps us humanize them. For the truth is "hurt people hurt people." When we, through prayer, are able to recognize that, oftentimes, people are difficult because they are hurting inside, it helps us gain understanding and sensitivity.

Respond respectfully. Now I want to give you a few guaranteed responses to difficult people that will disarm them in a respectful way. Not possible? It certainly is. Next time you are faced with a difficult person who speaks in a hurtful manner or says some inappropriate things, try these out: "That's interesting. Tell me more." "That's interesting. Why would you say that?" "That's interesting. Why would you ask that?" "I want to hear everything you have to say, just not in that manner." These responses have the potential to deflate the negative emotion in the room and draw attention to the unkindness, but in a respectful manner. Nine times out of ten, these responses will help get you out of a jam.

Compliment courageously. Okay, this may seem impossible to do, but it can work wonders. Next time you are faced with a difficult person, try to find something about them you appreciate and tell them. Why? Sometimes, people are difficult because they do not feel appreciated or valued. When they feel appreciated, oftentimes they release whatever resentment they are holding on to.

I remember a man at another church I served who caused much turmoil for me. It seemed he was against me from the start. If I voted yes, he voted no. If I voted no, he voted yes. He made things very difficult for me. I prayed, "Lord, help me deal with this man. What should I do?"

Shortly after I began praying for this man, there was a fall festival at the church. I walked around to the different booths, admiring the arts and crafts created by those in the congregation. The man I was praying for had a booth full of paintings he had done. They were portraits. I had no idea he was a painter, and a good one at that! I asked him to show me his paintings and tell me about them -- and he did, with great enthusiasm.

The next day, I sent him a note thanking him for showing me his paintings. I also told him how much I appreciated his gift for painting. I couldn't believe what happened next. He told everyone about the note and never gave me any more trouble. In fact, he became my biggest supporter!

That was a huge blessing to me! And that is what the Bible promises to us. We will inherit a blessing when we love the unlovely. The blessing may be a renewed relationship. The blessing may be being a witness of the love of Christ. The blessing may be recognizing the power of God working through you in a difficult situation. But there will always be a blessing when we choose to love the unlovely.

Imagine this world if every Christian decided to love the unlovely. Just imagine. We are never more like Christ than when we love the unlovely.

Amen.

Epiphany 4
1 Corinthians 1:18-31

How Will You Measure Your Life?

How will you measure your life? The world tells us we should measure our lives by how much money we have, what cars we own, the achievements we have made, and the power and status we have attained. But, in the end, is this really how we want to measure our lives? Is this how we want to be remembered?

Clay Christiansen wrote a great book titled, *How Will You Measure Your Life?* Christensen is a Harvard business professor who, surprisingly, tells his students that their lives should not be measured by their success in business.

Christiansen also graduated from Harvard, and he explains his experience attending class reunions. He said at his fifth year reunion, his fellow classmates seemed to be doing really well. They had high-paying jobs plus great marriages and families. Their lives seemed to be going well on every level.

But by the tenth reunion, he experienced something he never expected. Several of his successful classmates didn't come back for the reunion. As he asked other classmates where they were, he discovered that although many of his classmates were successful, they were not happy. Many of them had broken marriages. Some of them were already on their second marriages and had strained relationships with their kids. Their professional success had done nothing to help their personal misery.

Over the years, it didn't get any better. In fact, it got worse. Christiansen said at his twenty-fifth and thirtieth year reunions, he found out that one of his classmates had been sent to prison for white-collar crime. He was a stand-up guy in law school, but something sent him down the wrong path. But he wasn't the only one. Other classmates had gone down similar paths. One was arrested for insider training. Another ended up in jail for having a sexual relationship with a minor. Some of them were on their third and fourth marriages.

Christiansen tells his students this story every year as a cautionary tale. Do not measure your life by success, money, and achievement. Those things can be wonderful, but they will never bring real meaning and satisfaction to your life (Clay Christiansen, *How Will You Measure Your Life*, Harper Business, prologue, Kindle version).

Is this a message you need to hear? Perhaps you have received the awards, success, money, notoriety, power, recognition, praise, and glory. Yet you are still empty inside. There is a hole in you that cannot be filled. All the things you have done and achieved are not giving you the fulfillment you desired.

To help encourage you, let me give you a quiz I came across years ago. I am not sure of its source, but it's useful. I want you to try to answer these questions:

1. Name the five wealthiest people in the world.

2. Name the last five Heisman trophy winners.

3. Name the last five winners of the Miss America Contest.

4. Name ten people who have won the Nobel or Pulitzer Prize.

5. Name the last half dozen Academy Award winners for best actor and actress.

6. Name the last decade's worth of World Series winners."

How did you do? I am willing to bet you didn't do very well. "All glory fades."

Here's another quiz. See how you do on this one:

1. List a few teachers who aided your journey through school.

2. Name three friends who have helped you through a difficult time.

3. Name five people who have taught you something worthwhile.

4. Think of a few people who have made you feel appreciated and special.

5. Think of five people you enjoy spending time with.

It's easier to answer those questions, isn't it? What does that tell you? The people who make a difference in your life are not the ones with the most credentials, the most money, or the most awards. They are the ones who care. They are the ones who are faithful; who serve; who show unusual kindness and love.

The Bible has taught us this all along. God will measure our lives not by how much we get but by how much we *give*. Jesus told us that "*it is better to give than to receive"* (Acts 20:35 NRSV). He also said, *"Whoever loses their life, gives their life away for my sake will save it, will find life, but whoever holds on to their life for themselves, will lose life, will never find life. What good is it for someone to gain the whole world, and yet lose or forfeit their very self?"* (Luke 9:24-25 NRSV).

It's clear: Jesus tells us that God measures each of our lives by how much of it we are willing to give away for him — how well we love and how well we serve. This is not the world's idea of success, but don't forget that 1 Corinthians 1:18 reminds us: *For the message of the cross is foolishness to those who are perishing, but to us who are being saved it is the power of God(NIV).* Now why? Living a life of giving is the only way to find meaning and happiness in this world. If you are looking for fun, joy, meaning, and satisfaction, give your life away in service to Christ. The happiest people I know are the most generous people I know. And the most miserable people I know are the stingiest people I know. God hardwired us to be generous and joyful. We are made in God's image.

Another big reason why God measures our lives by how much we give is that when God wants something done in this world, he counts on us to do it! We are God's agents in the world. Take a look at this passage that spells it out:

> *God can pour on the blessings in astonishing ways so that you're ready for anything and everything, more than just ready to do what needs to be done… He gives you something you can then give away, which grows into full-formed lives, robust in God, wealthy in every way, so that you can be generous in every way, producing with us great praise to God* (2 Corinthians 9:8, 11 MSG).

God gives us something we can give away. And as we give it away, the more we get back -- so that we can continue to be generous. We are to be the channel through which God's blessings and power reach the world! As we receive blessings from God, we are to give those blessings away.

I am reminded of the parable of the rich fool in Luke 12. The man had accumulated much wealth and "stuff" and built bigger barns to hoard it. Jesus called him a fool -- not because he was rich, but because he didn't know why he was rich. It never dawned on him that he was blessed in order to be a blessing to others.

I read somewhere that there is only one incident in the Bible where God meets the needs of others without using his people. It was when God provided manna to the Israelites in the desert. However, the manna stopped once the people reached the promised land. Every other time God wanted to help others, he did it through his people. We are the hands and feet of Jesus in the world! We are the body of Christ in this world! What do we think that means?

When the people of God are not faithful, something God wants done does not get done. We are the only hands God has! When the people of God are silent when injustices occur across this world, something God wants done does not get done. We are the only voice God has!

When we ask God, "Why aren't you doing anything about all of this suffering?" God's response is, "I am and I have. I have given my people all the resources they need to change and heal this world. I will never stop giving blessings so you can be a blessing, so why aren't you doing anything about it?"

Look at the story of Jesus feeding 5,000 families in the wilderness in Mark 6. A big crowd was hungry. Jesus told the disciples to feed them. The disciples said, "What? We can't do that? Do you know how much money that would cost?" Well, Jesus ignored their excuses. Jesus said, "How many loaves do you have?" Mike Slaughter interpreted Jesus' question to mean, "Don't look at what you don't have, look at what you do have!"

The disciples found five loaves and two fish. Jesus told the disciples to seat the people on the grass and tell them to get ready for a feast. The disciples thought Jesus had lost his mind. Jesus blessed the bread and fish and fed 5,000 families with it.

You see, God blessed and multiplied what they had to give away. The disciples had enough faith in Jesus to give him what they had -- and he multiplied it! That's what God always does — when we give him what we have, he multiplies it so that there is more than we could ever imagine. In the story, after everyone is fed, there is such an abundance that there is more left over!

One day, God will say to us,:"I gave you the gift of this church. What did you do with it? I gave you the gift of music. What did you do with it? I gave you the gift of teaching. What did you do with it? I gave you the gift of preaching. What did you do with it? I gave you the gift of wealth and resources. What did you do with it?"

Jim Wallis reminds us, "Faith is personal but never private." The closer you get to Christ, the more he leads you to see the suffering that he sees and inspires you to help him! Jesus is out in the world begging us to help him lift up the weak.

I recall hearing Archbishop Desmond Tutu speak at Candler School of Theology many years ago. He said something in his sermon I will never forget: "So many

Christians just go to the foot of the cross and thank Jesus for what he has done. But very few Christians get up on the cross with Jesus to see what Jesus sees and to feel what Jesus feels. It is only when they do that they will be motivated and empowered to help Jesus heal this broken world."

Paul Tournier once said, "Every Christian needs two conversions — one out of the world, and one back into it." I believe that. The Christian faith is not only about personal piety, reaching up to God and reaching in to ourselves. The Christian faith is only complete when our reaching up and reaching in leads us to reach out to others.

I love what Bob Goff has to say about serving Christ in his book *Love Does*. He said the way he learned how to really serve Christ and love others was by quitting Bible study. That's right. He said he became a better Jesus follower when he quit Bible study. He said Bible study wasn't useful to him because he never applied what he learned. Eventually he would forget what he learned because he wasn't applying it.

Goff said about fifteen years ago, he began to get together with a group of guys each week and instead of calling it a "Bible study," they call it a "Bible doing." They simply read what the Bible has to say and then focus on what they are going to do about it. Goff says if you get engaged like that, you will be able to remember Bible verses because you are living them instead of just reading them (https://carolaround.com/2012/07/30/are-you-doing-the-bible/).

Bible doing instead of Bible studying — I like that! What if we called all of our Bible studies and Sunday school classes "Bible doings" instead of "Bible studies"? What if every group was required to ask, "Based on what we have learned this week, what are we going to do about it? How are we going to show unusual kindness to the beaten, broken, and bruised? How are we going to build a fire for those who are cold and tired? How are we going to be a source of light, warmth, and strength in a dark and cold world?" In the end, that is what matters.

This is what translates in our culture today. People have grown tired of religious trappings and talk. The world doesn't need another sermon; it needs servants. The world doesn't need another religious platitude; it needs caring people. The world doesn't need more Christians screaming in judgment; it needs people who will give a cup of cold water in Jesus' name. The world doesn't need more guilt laid upon it; it needs more people who will embody the love of Jesus. The world needs less Bible students and more Bible doers!

The world needs people who will rise above hate, cynicism, and complacency -- and penetrate this hurting world with loving service and sacrifice. That's when people will start wondering who Christians are and, more importantly, who Jesus is. That's when people will start asking us about Jesus and desiring a relationship with him. People don't respond to words; they respond to actions. And serving is putting God's love into action.

God will measure our lives by how well we have loved and served. Are you using the resources God has given you to do his work in the world? We are called to be God's agents of love. Let's get after it.

Amen.

How Does Prayer Work?

If you grew up in the church, I am sure you were taught that prayer is important. Even if you don't have much of a religious background, there is a good chance you have heard about the benefits of prayer. If you need something, ask God for it. If you need guidance, ask God for it. If you are worried, pray about it. If you need strength, pray for it.

But maybe you struggle with prayer because you never seem to get the results you are looking for. You pray and never seem to get an answer. You are frustrated because you hear people talking all the time about the power of prayer -- as if God is eating cornflakes with them at the breakfast table every morning -- and when you pray, it feels like you are ringing the doorbell to an empty house!

A colleague of mine tells of the time when he was helping paint the outside of his neighbors' home. His neighbor had a small black dog that had a ritual of going to the back door of the house. Once the little dog got to the back door, he would bark and bark until someone finally got the message and let him out.

One day, my colleague was painting the outside of this house when no one was home. The neighbor's dog ran to the back door and barked and barked all day long. The sad thing was that it never dawned in his little brain that all his barking was totally useless — no one was home to hear!

Ever felt that way about your prayers? You have prayed and prayed for something, but there seems to be no answer — there seems to be no one home!

Maybe you have a heavy burden in your life and you have prayed and prayed about it -- and you wonder if all your prayers have been falling on deaf ears. Maybe you have prayed for a troubled child, a sick relative, a job, a better marriage, or some other serious issue -- and you don't seem to be getting the answer you need. You wonder, "Is God listening?" And maybe you feel you are not doing it right, and you think if you come to the right church or sing the right song or say that right prayer, things will be different.

Perhaps you are skeptical about prayer. Maybe you think it is just wishful thinking or whistling in the dark. You think the whole idea of the Creator of the world listening to one prayer among billions is ridiculous. "Really? God has to listen to so many prayers! How does that work?"

Does prayer make any difference, or are we just wasting our breath? Well, so much of our frustration with prayer has to do with a lack of understanding of what prayer is. We have to understand what prayer is before we can know how it works. We can't get faith right until we get prayer right.

Let me begin by saying that prayer is not religious magic. People often believe that if they say the right phrases or have the proper technique, they can persuade God to answer their prayers.

There is an old story about a monk who was bothered by mice playing around him when he prayed. To stop it, he got a cat and kept it in his prayer room so the mice would be scared away. However, he never explained to his disciples why he had the cat. One day, the monk walked down the corridors of the monastery and noticed that each of his disciples had a cat in their prayer room. After seeing the monk with a cat, they thought that having a cat was the secret to powerful praying!

I believe this is a parable for many Christians today. Many believe they have to do something special in order for God to hear them and answer them. You will often see folks running here and there to learn the latest prayer gimmick from self-proclaimed spiritual gurus.

Prayer is not rubbing a magic lamp. It is not presenting some Santa Claus in the sky with a list of things we want. So what is prayer? I know that is the burning question for many of you today. How does prayer work?

Well, I know someone who has the answer. His name is Jesus. Jesus knew how about the power of prayer and how it worked. Take a look at this verse from Luke:

> *[Jesus] would withdraw to deserted places and pray* (Luke 5:16 NSRV).

In the gospel of Luke, we find fifteen different references to Jesus praying. Jesus taught us what prayer is by his own example. He prayed at every turn in his life. He prayed as he sensed God's call on his life; he prayed before choosing his disciples; he prayed as he served and healed other people; he prayed as he felt the demands and pressures of his ministry; he prayed as he faced the cross; he prayed as he finished his work on the cross. Jesus is continually praying. Prayer was as vital to Jesus as was taking his next breath. Jesus could not have accomplished what he did on earth without the power of prayer.

It was out of his own consistent prayer life that Jesus gave us a powerful lesson about prayer in Luke 11. The disciples notice Jesus praying frequently, and they finally get a clue and say, "Uh, Jesus, that prayer thing you are always doing? Can you teach us to do it too?" They observed that prayer was a vital practice for Jesus, and they wanted to learn how to do it. What follows is a profound lesson from Jesus about prayer:

> *And he said to them, "Suppose one of you has a friend, and you go to him at midnight and say to him, 'Friend, lend me three loaves of bread; for a friend of mine has arrived, and I have nothing to set before him.' And he answers from within, 'Do not bother me; the door has already been locked, and my children are with me in bed; I cannot get up and give you anything.' I tell you, even though he will not get up and give him anything because he is his friend, at least because of his persistence he will get up and give him whatever he needs"* (Luke 11:5-8 NRSV).

Notice that this was not a lesson in right technique. It was not a lesson in right phrasing. It was not a lesson in how to persuade God. It was a lesson in persistence. Through sharing the story of the man banging on the door all night, Jesus was telling us that effective prayer was consistent prayer. Effective prayer is a continual connection to God. For prayer to make a difference, it must become a habit. When conversation with God becomes a habit, we will be rewarded. Take a look at what Jesus said about it:

> *"So I say to you, Ask, and it will be given you; search, and you will find; knock, and the door will be opened for you. For everyone who asks receives, and everyone who searches finds, and for everyone who knocks, the door will be opened"* (Luke 11:9-10 NRSV).

You know what this means? This means that God always answers our prayers. Whenever we ask, God will answer. Whenever we search, we will find. Whenever we knock, God will open the door. And Jesus says this is true for everyone. Everyone who seeks God persistently in prayer will receive an answer. This is a spiritual law. God answers prayer.

But notice what Jesus does not say. Jesus does not say everyone who asks receives the answer they want; finds what they are looking for; or has the door they want open opened. God always answers us, but we may not always like the answer or expect the answer we receive. Effective prayer is not about what we can get from God, but what we receive from God. There is a big difference! For, often times, what we want from God and what we receive from God are two different things.

Perhaps this changes your wondering about unanswered prayer. Maybe God has answered you and you just don't like the answer. Someone once said that God answers prayer in one of four ways: "Yes," "no," "wait," and "are you kidding me?" I recall times in my own life when I prayed and prayed for God to give me something, yet my prayers were never answered, or so I thought. Later, I discovered that what I had wanted had not been right for me. That event always reminds me of the country song, "Thank God For Unanswered Prayer." There have been other times when God seemed to know that I was not ready for the answer to my prayer or the timing was not right; and God asked me to wait.

But Jesus clearly states that there is something we can always count on receiving from God when we pray. Listen closely:

"Is there anyone among you who, if your child asks for a fish, will give a snake instead of a fish? Or if the child asks for an egg, will give a scorpion? If you then... know how to give good gifts to your children, how much more will the heavenly Father give the Holy Spirit to those who ask him!" (Luke 11:11-13 NRSV).

This is the single most important text about prayer. Jesus says that whenever we seek God in prayer, God will always give to us his Spirit (the Holy Spirit). The purpose of the Holy Spirit is to love us, mold us, shape us, guide us, empower us, and direct us.

This means that prayer is not putting our order in to God. Prayer is not getting our phrasing right so we can unlock the God machine. Prayer is intimate conversation with God. It is as natural as turning around and speaking to a friend. It is also being quiet and still and listening to God, and being transformed by him.

Prayer is a conversation with God that brings us closer to God and allows us to be formed by his love. Prayer is intimacy with God.

So here is how prayer works -- (are you ready?) -- *Prayer does not change God; it changes us.* Prayer does not give us what we want from God; prayer helps us want what we need from God. I believe this is what Paul had in mind when he wrote in 1 Corinthians:

The Spirit searches all things, even the deep things of God. For who knows a person's thoughts except their own spirit within them? In the same way no one knows the thoughts of God except the Spirit of God. What we have received is not the spirit of the world, but the Spirit who is from God, so that we may understand what God has freely given us. This is what we speak, not in words taught us by human wisdom but in words taught by the Spirit, explaining spiritual realities with Spirit-taught words (1 Corinthians 2:10-13 NIV).

These profound words of scripture remind me of that old saying, "Prayer is not bending God's will to our will; it is bending our will to God's will."

I remember going on vacation with my family when I was a kid. Our resort was next to a big lake, and you could take canoes out on it. One morning, I decided to go canoeing. On my way back in, I accidentally dropped the oar in the water -- and the current took it away.

There I was, stuck in the middle of this lake. The current drifted me a little closer to the shore and I began to call out. Finally, a man saw me, grabbed a rope, threw it out to me, then tied the rope to the dock and told me to pull myself in. I got the feeling this was not the first time he had done this for a guest! As I was pulling on the rope, there was this optical illusion. It looked like I was pulling the dock to me, but in reality I was pulling myself closer to the dock.

This is what persistent prayer does. It does not move God to us. It pulls us closer to God. As we move closer to God in prayer, we find we are changed by his love and power. Prayer does not change God; it changes us.

So often, we forget this and pray, "Okay God, I don't need much of your time. You don't need to get too involved. Just give me some direction here. What should I do?" God replies, "Just hang out with me for a while. Let's spend some time together. I want to show you some things." We persist, "Lord, really. I don't need that much of you. Just give me a yes or no." God replies, "Just abide in me and my love from day to day, and you will find what you are looking for."

God still wants us to bring him our needs, our desires, and our questions and doubts. But God wants more than that. God wants us! God wants a relationship with us.

When I make prayer a habit, something happens on the inside of me. I become more sensitive to God's love in my life; and my motives and desires begin to change. For me, prayer allows the power and wisdom of God to break in -- and I begin to be transformed by God's love.

If you want to experience to power of prayer, I have a simple suggestion for you. If you do what I am about to tell you, you will experience the difference that prayer can make in your life. For the next seven days, start your day with prayer. It doesn't have to be a long time — five to ten minutes. You can stay in your bed, sit in a chair, or do it at the breakfast table. Get a devotional or turn to your favorite passage of scripture. Read the devotional or scripture passage. When you find that you are quiet on the inside, pray, "Lord, I want to get to know you better. I want to know your love. I want a relationship with you…" Then share with God what is on your mind and heart. Don't hold back. Just share it. He is listening and wants to hear from you. Prayer is simply a conversation with God. Be sure to include not only your own needs but also the needs of others. Then take a moment to listen in your heart to God, and write down what you sense God is saying to you. Before you end your prayer time, pray, "Lord, I want to please you. I want to do your will. Whatever it is you want, that's what I want too. I want to fit into your plans. Show me the way."

There is an old preacher's story about an organ in a large church that broke down one Sunday morning during worship. A member of the congregation happened to be an organ repairman and he rushed to the organ to fix it. He found that it was a simple electrical problem. When he finally got it fixed, it was just about the middle of the sermon. He quietly passed a note to the organist that read: "After prayer, the power will be on."

It's true: After prayer, the power will be on in your life. God is waiting to hear from you.

Amen.

*(This sermon was adapted from "I Wonder Why My Prayers Go Unanswered" in my book *Seven Wonders of the Faith: Answers to Our Most Troubling Questions*, Lima: Ohio, CSS Publishing Company, 2006, pages 23-28.)

Epiphany 6
1 Corinthians 3:1-9

When You're Out Of Tune

Bill Self wrote about a bluegrass radio station in Missouri that received a unique phone call. The caller said to the DJ, "Hello, I am a farmer living alone on my farm. My wife is dead. And my children and grandchildren have moved away; I don't see them very much. There are three things in my life that give me comfort: One is the farm. Second is my radio. The third is my fiddle. Sometimes in the night, when you are playing songs that I know and love, I get out my fiddle and play along with you. It brings me great comfort. But recently, my fiddle has gotten out of tune. The A string doesn't work like it should, and I don't have a tuning fork so there is no way I can get my fiddle back in tune. Would you mind playing the A note on your next program? If you will do this, I can tune my fiddle." So the station played the A note, and he tuned his fiddle, and all was right with the world (Bill Self, *Defining Moments*, Lima: Ohio, CSS Publishing Company, 1999, p. 19).

Fiddles are not the only things that can get out of tune. Churches can too. Churches can forget why they exist -- and play the wrong note in the world. It doesn't happen all at once. It is rather insidious. Church business slowly replaces the business of the church. Budgets concerns begin to override kingdom concerns. The past becomes more important than reaching people in the present. Without realizing it, a congregation settles for doing church rather than being the church. They are out of tune.

In the third chapter of 1 Corinthians, the apostle Paul was addressing a church that was out of tune. Their loyalties were divided. Jealousy was running rampant. Paul had this to say to them:

> *Brothers and sisters, I could not address you as people who live by the Spirit but as people who are still worldly — mere infants in Christ. I gave you milk, not solid food, for you were not yet ready for it. Indeed, you are still not ready. You are still worldly. For since there is jealousy and quarreling among you, are you not worldly? Are you not acting like mere humans? For when one says, "I follow Paul," and another, "I follow Apollos," are you not mere human beings?... For we are co-workers in God's service; you are God's field, God's building* (1 Corinthians 3:1-4, 9 NIV).

If the early church had problems staying in tune, it is certain that the church of today struggles with it.

You probably know the story about the little boy who went to church with his grandparents. His grandmother sat in the choir, and she often got irritated when grandfather nodded off to sleep in the middle of the sermon.

Finally, she decided on a plan. She gave her little grandson fifty cents each Sunday morning to poke grandpa in the ribs whenever he fell asleep. This plan worked until Easter morning. The church was packed. Grandmother was sitting in the choir. She noticed grandfather nodding off. However, Tommy just sat there and let granddaddy snore away.

After the service grandmother was very disappointed in Tommy. "Tommy," she said, "What happened? You knew I would pay you fifty cents after the service if you kept grandfather awake." Tommy replied, "Yes Ma'am, but grandfather offered me a $1 if I would let him sleep" ("A Service the Church Will Never Forget" by King Duncan, https://sermons.com/sermon/a-service-the-church-will-never-forget/1346997).

Some churches would rather just stay asleep than awake to the needs of the world. There may have been a day when they had been fine-tuned, blowing their trumpet for the gospel, but years of focusing on their power and agenda instead of on God has caused them to burnout. They would rather be left alone than be bothered with the mission of making disciples.

Some cynic said, "If it was up to some Christians, churches would have lightning rods on their steeples instead of crosses -- both in memory of that time when lightning struck the early church and as protection against it ever happening again."

So how does a church fine-tune itself? It plays the A note of the gospel of Jesus Christ. The church sings about it, preaches about it, prays about it, and talks about it. The church exists to make disciples of Jesus Christ for the transformation of the world. The church exists to spread the good news of God's redeeming love of Christ so that all people will come experience that love and learn to share that love with others. That's it. It is pretty simple, but it is amazing how the church, can complicate it, dilute it, or forget it.

Here are some key signs that a church is fine-tuned to the gospel of Jesus Christ:

Reaches Out More than It Reaches In

Jesus said, *"Go therefore and make disciples of all nations, baptizing them in the name of the Father ..., Son ... and Holy Spirit..."* (Matthew 28:19 NRSV).

Notice what Jesus did not say. He didn't say "Go therefore and sing your favorite songs in worship." He didn't say, "Go therefore and find a church you're comfortable with and attend twice a year." He didn't say "Go therefore and hang out with Christians who think like you." He said, "Go and make disciples of all nations." It is the Great Commission. Unfortunately, it has become the Great *Omission!*

Dr. Eugene Brice tells about a guy who toured the world's largest grease factory. "They walked through rows of machines with gears turning, wheels revolving, cylinders whirling, belts running, and huge motors roaring away. Toward the end of the tour, the guy asked the guide, 'What do you do with all the grease you make here? Do you sell it?' The guide said, 'Oh, no. We don't sell it. We have to use all the grease we produce to lubricate the machinery here at the factory'" (Duncan, "A Service the Church Will Never Forget," https://sermons.com/ sermon/a-service-the-church-will-never-forget/1346997).

Well, that'll preach! Churches quickly get out of tune when they put all of their energy and time in lubricating their own machinery and ignoring the needs of the community and the world. When a church starts ignoring the needs of the community and the world, it is "lights out" for that church.

Take a look at what the book of Acts says about the early church: *The number of those being added to the early church was increasing daily* (Acts 2:47). Why do you think the early church grew like wildfire? It is because they were constantly enlarging their fellowship. They were continually thinking of ways to reach the world for Jesus Christ.

Inwardly-focused churches die and outwardly focused churches thrive. I'll prove it to you. Go to any church that is dying and you will find people who are preoccupied with their history and the way they used to do things and why they can't change. They only see themselves. But go to any church that is growing and you will find people who are always thinking about how to reach people who aren't yet there. Those churches get it!

As someone once said, "The church is the only institution in the world that exists for the people who are not a part of it." We have the greatest job in the world. We get to tell people that God loves them and has a plan for them. Churches don't thrive until they begin living to reach the world that God so loves.

In addition to reaching out more than reaching in, a church is fine-tuned when it is inclusive rather than exclusive.

Inclusive Rather Than Exclusive

The apostle John said,

> *"For God so loved the world that he gave his one and only Son, that whoever believes in him shall not perish but have eternal life"* (John 3:16 NIV).

Once again, notice what Jesus does not say. He doesn't say, "For God so loved the beautiful people" or "the Christians" or "the Republicans" or "the Democrats" or "the United Methodists." It says, "For God so loved the *world*."

We have a myriad of denominations. We also have some churches that can't agree on any of the denominations, and so they sit alone as non-denominational churches. We have churches that determine who is in who is out by the kind of language people use about the inspiration

121

of scripture -- or how they worship; or how they read the Bible; or how they pray; or how they baptize; or, Lord have mercy, how they vote! While all this nonsense is going on, Christians are forgetting that Jesus said the world will know we are his by disciples not by how we worship, not by how we read the bible, not by how we pray, and not by the denomination we belong to, but by our love for one another.

I believe one of the biggest problems facing the church today is the disparity people experience when interacting with Christians who preach love but act hateful. 1 John is clear that it is impossible to love God and hate another person. If we hate another person, then we need to examine whether we understand the love of God.

Yes, we must evangelize. Yes, we must be working to make disciples, but we have no right to act arrogantly or exclusively. Remember that in the New Testament, God in Jesus is going to the ungodly. In Jesus' stories, it is the religiously wrong who get praise. The Good Samaritan is religiously wrong, has the wrong version of the scripture, and worships improperly -- but in Jesus' story, he is closer to the kingdom. In Matthew 8, it is the pagan centurion who has faith greater than any Jesus had seen in Israel.

Watch out in the New Testament! The outsiders become the insiders, and the worst of Jesus' judgments are on those religious folks who think they are the only insiders (Matthew 23). The closer we follow Jesus, the more accepting and loving we are to all people. We must hope for the best for them because God claims them too. Christ died for them too. And, as the Bible makes perfectly clear, there are surprises at the judgment. In Matthew 25, it is those who feed the hungry and clothed the naked that are saved. In Romans 11, Paul makes it clear that all Isreal will be saved. If Christ died for them, if there is hope for them; if God is going to treat them the same way he treats us then we better treat them in the same way, hoping that they also will be in the kingdom. Madeleine L'Engle said that our job is to reflect to others "a light so lovely that they will want to know with all their hearts the source of it."

If a church is in tune, it will reach out more than reach in. It will be inclusive rather than exclusive. Most of all, it will show mercy instead of judgment.

Show Mercy Instead Of Judgment

Jesus said,

> *"Do not judge, and you will not be judged. Do not condemn, and you will not be condemned. Forgive, and you will be forgiven. Give, and it will be given to you. A good measure, pressed down, shaken together and running over, will be poured into your lap. For with the measure you use, it will be measured to you"* (Luke 6:37-38 NIV).

> *"Be merciful, just as your Father is merciful"* (Luke 6:36 NIV).

One of the problems with Christians and churches today is they get angry with certain people simply because they sin differently than they do. Too many Christians today are known for their judgment instead of for their mercy. They are known for their hatred instead of for their love for one another. Many non-Christians see Christians as hypocritical, judgmental, heartless, arrogant, and close-minded. That doesn't sound like Jesus, does it?

I once heard about a preacher who worked very hard trying to convert an atheist to Christianity. She was a young adult with a sharp mind. This preacher presented argument after argument to her, but she wouldn't budge. Finally, he got word that she had converted to Christianity. The preacher was thrilled. He called her up and asked proudly, "Which thing did I say that convinced you? What argument did it?" She replied, "Sorry, you are not the one who convinced me. No argument convinced me. What moved me to be a Christian were my Christian friends who loved me and never judged me. I saw Jesus in them, and I wanted what they had."

We will be in tune as a church when we reach out more than we reach in, when we are inclusive rather than exclusive, and when we show mercy instead of judgment.

Amen.

Why Doesn't God Prove Himself To Doubters?

If you've ever doubted God's existence or know someone who has, this message is for you. If you are afraid to express your struggles with faith, this message is for you. The truth is, 99% of us are in one of those categories, and 1% is lying. So this message is for everyone!

I have gone through seasons of doubt. It's called being human. It is normal. I wouldn't be much of preacher if I didn't struggle with doubt. I wouldn't have much to offer. I believe with Frederick Buechner that "doubts are the ants in the pants of faith; they keep it alive and moving."

There is more faith in doubt than you might think. John Wesley said that doubt is the front porch to faith. You show me someone who has never gone through seasons of doubt, and I'll show you someone with a shallow faith.

Here's a question that reflects a common struggle of faith: Why can't God do something spectacular for those who doubt him? "God, if you exist, give me a hole in one on this next golf hole!" Why can't God just skywrite a message that says, "I love you!" signed, "God"? Or, how about God doing a world tour, appearing in every city with a message for the world: "I do exist!" Ever wondered why God doesn't do something spectacular like that? It would remove all of our doubts and silence skeptics and cynics.

When British philosopher Bertrand Russell was asked what he would say if, after death, he found himself confronted by God, Russell replied, "I would say, `Why didn't you prove yourself to those who doubted you?'"

A clever comedian once said that he would have no difficulty believing in God: "All God would have to do would be to deposit $1,000,000 in my bank account." Unfortunately, God does not operate that way. Many believe that God has left no evidence or proof that he exists.

The writer of 2 Peter would beg to differ. In the following text, we are reminded of those who were eyewitnesses to the powerful works of Christ:

> *For we did not follow cleverly devised stories when we told you about the coming of our Lord Jesus Christ in power, but we were eyewitnesses of his majesty. He received honor and glory from God the Father when the voice came to him from the Majestic Glory, saying, "This is my Son, whom I love; with him I am well pleased." We ourselves heard this voice that came from heaven when we were with him on the sacred mountain* (2 Peter 1:16-18 NIV).

Although I was not an eyewitness to the works of Christ, I have been a witness to the glory and power of God all around me. When I think about the moment my son was born, or when I look at a sunset or gaze at the stars, I ask, "What more proof of God do we need than that?" All we have to do is look at the glory of creation to see that there is a God. Theologians call this the design argument. When we look at wonders around us, we conclude that all of it did not occur by chance. There has to be a Designer.

However, there are some who are not so sure. I had a friend in college who had a very strong faith. He grew up in a good Christian home and was very active in his church. He began his freshman year determined to hold onto his faith. He was exposed to new knowledge of science and biology. He also learned from the religion department that there were different ways to interpret the Bible and faith. It wasn't long before many doubts crept in. These doubts led him to give up his faith. Today, he has embraced the faith again and is active in a church but he still has many doubts and questions.

My friend reminds me of the man who came to Jesus with his sick boy in the gospel of Mark. He said to Jesus, "I believe; help my unbelief." If we are honest, that's where most of us live. There are days when we feel like Jesus is holding our hand, and there are days we feel completely in the dark.

If you struggle with doubts and questions about God's existence, you're in good company. The Bible is filled with people who doubted God. One of the famous doubters in scripture doubted so much that doubting became his first name — "Doubting" Thomas. His signature scene appears in the chapter 20 of John. Appearances of the resurrected Jesus were happening everywhere. Most of the disciples had encountered him, but not Thomas. Here is what Thomas had to say about that:

> *But Thomas (who was called the Twin), one of the twelve, was not with them when Jesus came. So the other disciples told him, "We have seen the Lord." But he said to them, "Unless I see the mark of the nails in his hands, and put my finger in the mark of the nails and my hand in his side, I will not believe"* (John 20:24-25 NRSV).

At one time or another, we have felt like Thomas: "Unless I see in his hands the print of the nails, and place my finger in the mark of the nails, and place my hand in his side, I will not believe." Maybe today, you wish God would just prove himself in some way.

Thomas got his wish. Take a look:

> *A week later his disciples were again in the house, and Thomas was with them. Although the doors were shut, Jesus came and stood among them and said, "Peace be with you." Then he said to Thomas, "Put your finger here and see my hands. Reach out your hand and put it in my side. Do not doubt but believe." Thomas answered him, "My Lord and my God!"* (John 20:26-28 NRSV)

Wouldn't you love to have that experience? "Finally! He showed up. I see proof with my own eyes. Now I believe!" But notice what Jesus said next:

> *Jesus said to him, "Have you believed because you have seen me? Blessed are those who have not seen and yet have come to believe"* (John 20:29 NRSV).

Why would Jesus make that statement? "Blessed are those who have not seen and yet have come to believe." It would make more sense if Jesus had said, "How noble and amazing are those who come to believe without proof." But that is not what he said. He said they were "blessed." Why would those who believe without proof be blessed? Because experiencing God goes much deeper than experiencing proof. It goes beyond the physical. Those who experience God beyond what can be seen by the eyes are truly blessed because they experience God on a deeper level.

God is a not a science experiment. God is a personal being. God is not an object to be observed; God is a spiritual power to be experienced. How do I know that? Well, let me share a few reasons why I believe this:

Proof Of God Doesn't Guarantee Belief In God

It's impossible for God to prove his existence. Why? Because God gave us the freedom to think. Any so-called "proof" God might give the world would be explained away by skeptics. For example, let's say God did send a comet in the sky to write to the world, "I love you, God." Or say God toured the world like Elvis and gave a show filled with miracles and wonders. You would still have folks who would not believe there is a God. Instead, they would say:

> — *The people witnessing the demonstration were hallucinating or dreaming* — *The demonstration was an optical illusion or a freak occurrence of atmospheric conditions*
> — *The demonstration is natural phenomena which science will eventually explain* — *The demonstration was not caused by God, but by someone else, possibly someone masquerading as God*
> — *The demonstration was misinterpreted: Aliens made a mistake when they tried to contact us, the scientists who documented it made mistakes or were biased towards theism, etc.; also,* (https://www.rationalchristianity. net/proof.html).

Regardless of what God tried to do to prove his existence, some folks would still find some way to refute it. So, proof of God doesn't always guarantee a belief in God.

129

Proof Does Not Always Lead To Faith

Many make the assumption that if God showed up and proved he existed to everyone, then all would be right with the world. Your Uncle Billy would stop drinking and come to church. Your atheist friend would convert and become a preacher. Sorry to burst your bubble, but proof of God does not always lead to faith in God. The Bible says, "Even the demons believe and tremble."

We must remember that there were many people in the Bible who witnessed miracles but did not follow God. Countless people witnessed the miracles of Jesus and yet fell away when things got tough.

I like how rationalchristianity.net puts it: "Even if God provided proof that was satisfactory to everyone, faith and trust would still be required to follow God. The atheist's question would merely change from 'Why doesn't God prove his existence?' to 'Why doesn't God explain why he did this and not that?' Atheists themselves might come to believe in a higher power, but not all of them would become Christians: one can believe God exists without believing he's worthy of worship, or that Christ saved us from sin" (https://www.rationalchristianity.net/proof.html).

Faith Is An Inside Job

A relationship with God must take place on a spiritual level. It can't happen on the outside of you. It must happen on the inside. Faith is an inside job. God communicates to us personally and intimately. God relates to each of us individually.

In his message "Learning to Doubt Our Doubts," King Duncan said, "This means you cannot find God with the most powerful telescope ever built. You cannot find him with a slide rule, a test tube, or an enormous computer. There is only one way to find God and that is to take a step of faith, and entrust your life to him... Could I prove to you that love exists? A scientist could attach electrodes to the skin of a person in love and measure the pulse, the respiration, and the blood pressure of a person in the presence of their beloved. But that would not prove love. Too much caffeine that morning at breakfast might cause the same bodily reactions. The only way you and I can ever prove love is to experience it — to love and be loved" (https://sermons.com/sermon/learning-to-doubt-our-doubts/1346993).

So it is with faith, by which we experience God. The only way to truly experience the reality of God is by trusting him with your life and by developing a relationship with him. The reality of God begins with an intimate connection with him and his love. The prophet Jeremiah puts it this way: *When you search for me, you will find me; if you seek me with all your heart* (Jeremiah 29:13 NRSV). A relationship with God must be based on trust, not proof. *Belief in God based on proof is a science experiment. Faith in God based on trust is a relationship.*

Maybe this is starting to make sense, but you still have your doubts and you don't know what to do with them. Let me lift up a passage of Scripture for you from the gospel of John, chapter 6. People are hearing Jesus teach and preach and they find his teachings difficult. More and more people are leaving him. It was fun for a while -- but then Jesus started getting more challenging in his teachings, and doubt crept in. Verse 66 says, *"Because of this many of his disciples turned back and no longer went about with him."* So there were doubts, struggles, and questions by many -- and some decided not to follow Jesus anymore. Sometimes doubts can do that to people. They allow their doubt to take over their lives, and they stop believing in God. They become bitter about the church and religion. And that is where you may be today -- and that's okay. God still believes in you even if you don't believe in him. But notice what happens next in the text:

> So Jesus asked the twelve, "Do you also wish to go away?" (John 6:67 NRSV).

Jesus saw everyone deserting him and he turned to the twelve and said, "Everyone's leaving me. What about you? You want to leave me too?" Simon Peter replied with the wisest answer anyone could give:

> "Lord, to whom can we go? You have the words of eternal life" (John 6:68 NRSV).

Now, sit with Peter's response for just a moment. Here is what I believe was going on inside the heart of Peter: When everyone else had chosen to walk away from Jesus, he thought about leaving too. I am sure he had his doubts. But perhaps he began to ask, "Where are they going? Who or what are they going to follow? What are they going to put their hope in? What are they going to put their trust in? Who are they going to put their faith in? In themselves? In others? In the Roman government? In pleasures? Jesus is the only one who can hold water! He is the only one I can really lean on!" So he said, "Lord, where else can I go? Where else can we go? You have the words to life. There is only you! I may have questions and doubts -- but there is only you."

When I have gone through periods of doubt and questioning, I remember Peter's words: "Where else can I go?" I can't go to anyone else! Who else can give me life!

The key question in the midst of doubt is, "Who or what will I follow?" Think that through. Doubt God; struggle; get angry; search. It is good for you. But before you make the ultimate decision to abandon your faith, ask: To whom or what will you go? Think about that. What is really going to satisfy you? What is really going to help you discover the truth about your life? What is really going to give you meaning? There is only God. He is the answer to all your questions and doubts. "To whom can you go?"

A cynical young medical student confronted a pastor: "I have dissected the human body," he announced, "and I found no soul." The pastor said, "That's interesting. When you dissected the brain, did you find a thought? When you dissected the eye, did you find vision? When you dissected the heart, did you find love?" The student answered thoughtfully, "No, I did not." The pastor replied gently, "Of course you believe in the existence of thoughts, of vision, and of love. The human soul is the totality of man's existence in relationship with God. Just because you cannot locate it on a medical chart does not mean that it does not exist" (*Frustrated by Their Lack of Faith* by King Duncan, https://sermons.com/sermon/frustrated-by-their-lack-of-faith/1348197).

When we stop searching for proof of God on the outside and begin to seek an experience of God on the inside, we will find all the proof we need.

Amen.

CPSIA information can be obtained
at www.ICGtesting.com
Printed in the USA
FFHW020621121219
56854545-62516FF